Daily Doses of Inspiration
Volume 1: For Spiritual Seekers

By Acacia Lawson

Copyright © Acacia Lawson, 2022
Cover design: Acacia Lawson
Editor: Stephen Elliot

All rights reserved. This book or parts thereof may not be reproduced in any form, stored in any retrieval system, or transmitted in any form by any means—electronic, mechanical, photocopy, recording, or otherwise—without prior written permission of the author, except as provided by United States of America copyright law.
For permission requests, write to the author at www.byacacia.com.

The information given in this book should not be treated as a substitute for professional medical advice; always consult a medical practitioner. Any use of the information in this book is at the reader's discretion and risk.
The author cannot be held responsible for any loss, claim, or damage arising out of the use, or misuse, of the suggestions made, the failure to take medical advice or for any material on third-party websites, books or movies.

For my husband –
You are my person, my Divine Counterpart and my best friend.
You encouraged me to start and finish this book, despite my 'nonsense' ☺
I am forever grateful for you.

Introduction

This book was created to offer motivation in the form of quotes and short stories written by the author on her social media pages and to her clients personally via messaging.

Each text was given to her from spirit (the universal consciousness, god source, higher self, etc.) in order to help other seekers on their spiritual journey - to keep the faith and to keep going!

At the end of each section, there is a "To-Do List" that will assist the reader in asking the hard questions to your own self, and discovering more of your truth.

She hopes that her words of encouragement will reach you on the days when you need them the most, and inspire you to reach for the stars no matter what!

"This is your life, this is your creation, and this is your time to shine!" – Acacia Lawson

Daily Doses of Inspiration
Volume 1: For Spiritual Seekers

Contents

Introduction 5

Conscious Creation 9

Health and Body 63

Internal Healing 91

Love 139

Soul Mission / Purpose 179

About the Author 231

Inspiration for Conscious Creation (a.k.a. Manifestation)

Taking the time to understand that our thoughts and feelings create our reality is one of the most important things we can do for ourselves.

We create our lives and we are responsible for our own happiness, love, and fun. This planet was designed to be a beautiful place where humans can freely express their innermost being - be it art, business, human interaction, nature worship, or anything they feel in their bones.

Once we remember our power, conscious creation becomes secondhand nature to us. But it is up to us to clear the way in order for this to happen.

For the highest good of all.

Are you a seeker?
Or are you sitting in your denial, stuck in your old patterns, wondering why everyone else gets their dreams and you're still in the same place that you were last year?

* * *

We write our own stories
Each chapter will vary.
There will be happiness, success, love.
Also sorrow, fear, worry, and loss.
This is the human experience.
And each time we think we know the end – we don't.
The good thing is, we can always edit it.
We can start over, again and again,
and we can always decide on each chapter's ending.
Follow your true calling and remember you are a soul having this human experience.
You create your life.
This is your power.

* * *

You choose to know your truth and act on it.
Nobody else can do that for you.
How are you living?
Are you where you want to be, in the relationship you want to be in, with the work/career you want to have?
What's your truth?

* * *

If you don't inspire yourself, what are you doing?
Reminder: You are a leader. Keep going!

* * *

"What is the hardest task in the world? To think." –
Ralph Waldo Emerson
[To think for one's self]
Your thoughts can alter the world – and help you create your reality.
What are you thinking and believing?
Who are you allowing to speak into your ear?

* * *

We're not out here trying to live a "normal" life.
We are creating the lives our souls desire, traveling wherever and whenever we want, and being the truest expression of ourselves.
This is living :)

* * *

Are you still second-guessing about releasing yourself from the heaviness that clings and is dragging you down?
Do you allow your relationship ties and societal norms to stop you from becoming who you really want to be?
Open up.
Embrace the new era.
Transform into your true authentic self!

* * *

To live in our true authentic self, living our true soul calling, is the most rewarding gift we can give ourselves.
As humans, we were taught to follow societal norms which most of the time, we tend to lose some of ourselves, parts of our soul.
Are you listening to your soul, or to the "demands" of others?

* * *

When we live the life we think we should live, we stop living the life we want to live.
We are the Author of our book, the Director of our movie, the Creator of our happiness.
Don't let anybody tell you differently.

* * *

<u>You Create Your Reality</u>.
What are you creating?
What are you speaking out loud?
What are you thinking but not voicing?

Will you go after what you truly desire, or live being told it's impossible or won't work for you?
You are the only person limiting yourself.
Not what's happening outside of you.
Not the lies you're being fed.

Tap into your soul, into your power, into your true essence.
See what comes up, and know that you have infinite power to create your reality.

It's just a question of if you're too scared of what others might think to actually do the work and make it happen. And "doing the work" always begins with working on yourself first.

I'm saying this because I'm doing it.
Creating my own reality.

I lived in/moved to three different countries across the globe in the second half of 2020 (supposedly impossible to do), traveled even more in 2021 (even though "nobody was flying"), laughed until I cried, met amazing people, and even hit a few bucket list items.
I keep on living from my future self.

That doesn't mean I've stopped doing the work on myself, my relationships, and my business.
I keep creating my reality.
Always.

* * *

The soul's true message is in all of us, yet very few realize and acknowledge it.
Because surrendering our physical self to our soul's true calling requires a lot of inner work, sacrifices, and courage.

How can you live the life that you desire, or be the person you want to be, if you're afraid of letting go of your old habits, of your old self, of your old beliefs, of negative people, of things and places that no longer serve your highest good?

* * *

You can create the life you dream of - the job, the business, the partner, the love, all of it.
Mindset is important.
What is yours?

* * *

Once you control your thoughts, and you live from that future self, the energy you are putting out comes back to you in physical form.

If you put out negativity (i.e. this is the way it is, this is who I am, it will never change, etc.), that's what you get back.

Switch the mind to positivity (i.e. that's who I was but now I am...., I am a natural born..., I love my clients/work....) and believe it 100%.

Stick with it for 21 days.
And watch your world change.

* * *

Where is your biggest resistance or fear regarding your business or personal life?
You need to look at that resistance/fear, ask it where it's really from and why it's there, and then take action on it immediately.

Trust your higher self.
Take the action!

* * *

Are you expressing your creativity?
What's your creative outlet?
How do you let your soul out?
It is essential for you to give voice to your soul by allowing your creative side to come out and play.

Make time for it.
Revel in the moment of creating.
This is where the liberation of staying present is witnessed.

* * *

<u>There is no end to the lengths We are Willing to Go.</u>
No risk we are not going to take.
No fight with our ego for control.

Once we are aligned and awakened to our soul's purpose on the earth at this time, we do all we are called to do.

We are led by our higher self, our intuition.
It never leads us astray and is our guiding light in this murky 3-D illusion.

Then we find we are creating heaven on earth.

The only pain felt is by our human integrating to the massive shifts we have chosen in faith, led only by god source.

For our mission here, at this time and in this realm, was written long ago. We wrote it.

There is no fear.
There is no worry or anxiety.

Only joy and love, acceptance and allowing.

We are protected and provided for.

We are warriors of light and truth, spreading our strength and vision, love and healing, and caressing those that have longed for this blossoming into who they truly are.

Don't lose faith. Stay the course.

Follow what you are shown and remember you are a soul having this human experience.

You create your life.
This is your power.
Now is your time!

* * *

Show us your mission, your dreams, your heart.
And we will stand with you in creating, in truth, and with love.

* * *

If you don't have 100% blind faith and acceptance,

it (what you desire to manifest/create)
is not going to happen
when you want it to or at all.

* * *

If you want something, you have to give up something
(sacrifice) →
money, time, energy, old habits, people.

In order for that something to manifest,
it must be aligned with your highest good;
you must say 'hell yes!' to it,
throw yourself into focusing on it and
then take the aligned steps towards it.

Once you have taken the aligned steps, you release it and allow.
This is conscious creation.

* * *

Don't be so hard on yourself.
Make allowances for minor delays and detours.
You are equal to these challenges,
and growth comes from here.

This is power!

* * *

Always ask yourself this before doing anything (place your hand on your heart and breathe deeply three times):

Is this opportunity something my heart, my higher self,
wants me
to be, do, or have?
#intuition

* * *

What you spend your free time doing shows up
in how your creativity and life are expressed.

What are you doing in your free time?
How much joy are you feeling?

* * *

If we are not in a nurturing environment,
we cannot freely grow and express our authentic selves.
We want to see your true self.
Get where you need to be so that we can see your ideas,
inventions, love, and beauty.

* * *

Get out of your own way.
Stop. Breathe.
Go with the flow and let the magic unfold.

Stop for one hour - stop being busy. Simply allow and be
still.

* * *

Don't let cynicism ("realism") kill your magic (dreams).

* * *

Reminder: you are who you surround yourself with.
Yes, even on social media.

* * *

There is more than enough love, joy, peace, money, ideas, creativity to go around.
There is no scarcity or lack.

We don't all want the same things or experiences.
That's the beauty of this human life!

* * *

Check in on your thoughts today.
Thoughts become things - circumstances, people, etc.
What are you thinking?

* * *

Everyone can, but only some do.
Vision without action is only a dream.
Aligned action, from your deep belief in the outcome, creates your reality.
#beliefandaction

* * *

Is your routine killing your intuition and opportunities?
Do you allow the universe to give you miracles?

* * *

I dare you to stop fumbling around with your dreams
and to go full speed ahead.

How many excuses will you have before you change your
normal pattern and instead do what scares you and
excites you simultaneously?

The only tragedy would be to stay small,
to not rock the boat, to not be as great as you can be.

Stop holding yourself back.
You were meant for more!

* * *

<u>Isolation helps you become crystal clear…</u>
On what you are on this earth to do.

You can see the years you wasted chasing other people's
dreams.

Now you have the chance to do what turns you on.
To follow your true self up the path meant for you.
To wake up every day ignited and excited.

Will you take it or will you keep running in the same
circle? Keep checking that list off of socially acceptable
things for you to be?

Walking around in zombie land with no energy or passion for life.

Keep playing it small or take the chance on yourself?

When you come out of this isolation, you have the opportunity to step into a whole new reality.

One that you created.
One that you shaped using your dreams and desires instead of your fears, shame, and guilt.

What are you waiting for?

The only thing or person holding you back is YOU.

Break the fear cycle.
Stop playing small.

Invest in yourself.

Live the life you always wanted!
Now is your time.

* * *

Sometimes, we forget the beauty around us.
Stop for a moment and be grateful
for the first thing you see.
Gratitude is an underrated super boost of energy!

* * *

You have all of the answers inside of yourself.
Take the time to ask and receive the truth.
You are more powerful than you give yourself credit for.
Keep on shining, you magnificent being!

* * *

<u>"You lack nothing. Use what I gave you. – God Source"</u>

Very few people are willing to put in the effort, faith, and persistence in order to have the life that we all can live - the joyful, loving, exciting, and abundant life.

Deep down in their souls, everybody knows what it takes to get there but they refuse to put in the effort.

For those of you putting in the effort of healing, strengthening, building the new earth (systems), and trusting, I see you.

I'm behind you and we rise together.

For those of you feeling less than, tired of life, repeating the same drama, or waiting for some miraculous savior or rapture, we are waiting for you to join us.

We have paved the less traveled road for you.
Reach out and ask us how.
Let's get this show on the road.

We are the effort we put in.
We are bringing all the love and all the feels.
We are creating this new earth together.

We are the future and we are here, now.

* * *

Reminder:
You don't have to tell anybody what you are doing until after it is done.
Keep your energy and your goals clear.

* * *

If you are not surrounded by encouraging and inspirational people,
it's time to move.

* * *

I hope you do what you are called to do today
(rest, take action, pray, etc).

What is meant for you will never pass you by →
but only you can take action on your soul's guidance.

* * *

<u>Your Words</u>
When you speak out loud, you cast a spell with your words (spell - ing).

This can be either positive or negative, but every word creates something.

How are you speaking about yourself (even as a joke) and about others?
Is it positive or negative?

Are you creating more good, love, and truth in the world or upholding outdated beliefs of judgment, hate, and fear?

We are in an accelerated timeline and our words create physically what is in our minds.
Try to speak from your heart.

That is the world we want to create together.

Much love to you and yours.

* * *

It's Your Decision
It's simple, really.

You can focus on the negative, the past, what happened to you or what someone did and that's why you do what you do now -> and you will keep creating more of that.

Or

You can focus on the positive, the future, and present, and being the best you can be (your highest self), and fulfilling your mission here -> and you will create more opportunities to take action on that, which will put you on your highest timeline.

Make no mistake - you must empty yourself in order to live as your highest self:

Reprogram your brain to think positively, retrain your subconscious to feel what you truly deserve, clear the trauma and ancestral line, and do the hard work that you need to do for your mission and self.

Because if you don't and you keep wishing for some rapture, some savior, for your own death so that you can go to heaven, and you continue living in fear and playing it small/not using your gifts that you were born with -> you will be coming back to do this again.

You agreed to a specific mission with god source. You agreed to come here at this time to not only liberate yourself, but to do this energetically for the collective.

So either you do it now, or you come back.

Either you drop all the crap: the judgements, the excuses, the fears, the lies, the trauma drama.

Or you die and get to do it all over again.

Those are your true choices.

So take the bull by the horns and get your rodeo started.

Or

Keep not doing the work and being miserable/playing it safe and we will see you down here again until you decide you're going to fulfill your god given mission.

* * *

Write down three intentions (goals, ideas, etc.) today that you want to happen in the next month,
six months and year.

Say them out loud firmly and joyfully three times.

Feel in your body that you have already accomplished them.
Give thanks for them!

Then take the inspired action.

* * *

<u>What's wrong with me?</u>

Feeling like the victim –
that you have no other options?
That you have to keep putting up with everything?
That you are powerless to your job, your relationship(s), your situation?

Feeling like 'what is the point'?

Feeling worn out from living?
Exhausted from the struggle and not quite sure what you're even struggling for at this point?

I felt like that too —
in NYC, wondering if this was all there was to life ->
work, sleep, eat, maybe see friends on the weekends, and feel bored/stressed out/sad/anxious/depressed/exhausted and dependent on stimulants (caffeine, booze, sugar, etc.) to keep me going.
I was doing yoga, meditation, reading self-help books, and trying to figure it out.
I tried veganism and became vegetarian.

But all of that wasn't working.

I still felt that something was missing.

That something was wrong with me.

Why wasn't I happy? Why wasn't I fine with a "normal life"?
Why did I want more - more fun, more joy, more travel, more of a community of like-minded souls?

Why couldn't I just do what everyone else did and just get through the day?

Because I (my soul) refused to be told what to do or how to live my life.

I refused to be controlled and to not live the kind of joyful life that I could see so clearly in my imagination.

I stopped playing the victim and started being proactive.

I moved myself out of NYC after 11 years, leaving behind a career, old life, and friends.

I hired coaches, energy healers, and psychics. I healed myself from my ancestral/generational trauma. I stopped drinking coffee and booze. I cut people out of my life who didn't fit my new vibe and what I was trying to achieve. I started setting boundaries. I retrained my brain and subconscious. I started discerning people's energy to keep users/takers away from me.

I met new friends and teachers. I uncovered more of my healing gifts and rediscovered my artistic joy of oil painting and writing. I reunited my divine masculine and feminine inside of me so that I didn't pass on unhealthy relationship issues, among other things.

And this opened up a whole new world for me! The opportunities started coming from everywhere. I simply had to be ready and act on them.

I began coaching people to heal their own traumas, to leave jobs/relationships/situations that no longer resonated, to rediscover their amazing gifts and their power within themselves, to truly love themselves and to live their soul mission(s).

I started writing my first book as my divine feminine (my intuition) instructed me. I self-published it in December 2020.

I began a beautiful, soul love relationship with the man that I am now married to.

I was painting again after 15 years of not.

I traveled more than I thought I would and have seen wonderful places and met amazing people.

This is only one part of my story. The best is yet to come but it's been one hell of a ride so far.

And why am I telling you this?

Because it's time to stop letting life happen to you. It's time to take back your power. Take back your control.

Stop playing the victim, the martyr, the poor child, or lonely adult or big baby. Stop pretending it's everyone else's fault your life is like it is.

YOU are the reason your life is like it is.

But you get to take back your power and say "Enough. It's time for a new way of living. A new way of being. A new beginning and chapter for my life."

YOU get to say "I'm ready today!!"

And that's the first step.

The next step is to take action on what comes up in your head after you tell the universe you're ready -> then go do it!

Then strap in and buckle up, and get ready for the wild, amazing, roller coaster of you (your mind, body, and soul) creating your life!

* * *

It is time to build the communities and systems you want to see.

Based in love and compassion, truth and wisdom, healing and communion with nature.

How are you taking steps towards this in real (physical) life? Not just the imagining and affirming it…

* * *

If you are "too busy" and constantly running around all day, you are not consciously creating your life.

You are allowing drama and negativity.
You get to choose: create your life or let it happen to you.

* * *

One day, every human will realize
the unlimited power within themselves,
and only be guided by love and truth.
One day.
For the highest good of all!

* * *

<u>How to Find Your Calling</u>
When I first started writing my book, I had no idea it was my calling.

I had dreamed of writing books since I was little, reading Jane Austen barefoot perched on a beloved tree branch in my childhood yard in Kansas.

I had loved writing until college when my English professor told me that I was a spoiled little rich girl (I was working three jobs and had scholarships lol), made fun of me in front of the entire class for writing differently, and made me doubt my writing, thus doubting myself and my dreams.
So I stopped writing.

I wrote little stories here and there about my jobs or New York City experiences while living there for 11 years, but I did nothing with them. They sat in a hidden folder on my computer desktop and I only rediscovered them this year.

Living in Bali and going through intense healing, meltdowns, building an online business and more, my intuition urged me to get off my yoga mat and write what was being downloaded in May 2020.

"You will write your first book and call it 'My Past Lives and How They Came Back to Haunt Me'. It will be about your past lives."

And then I was hit with a vision. Then another.

I wrote everything down as directed (although my ego argued a bit and said I wanted to write about self-development or love lol) in streams of consciousness.

Then I started paying past life regressionists to take me back to more past lives.

These regressions unlocked so many more gifts in me along with past life memories, and I wrote many more chapters in my book.
Then I started doing the regressions on myself.
And here I am today with a finished book, having moved to five other countries after Bali while I continued writing the book and coaching clients.

I published my book - my first dream as a child - after much editing, taking Amazon lessons, and being led by my intuition to hire the right people for specific things that were done so that my energy remained focused on creation.

I have consciously created this - slower than I (my ego) wanted yet my energy remained steady.

One year and a half later, 'My Past Lives' is taking on a life of its own, I'm a happily married woman, and I am walking my talk by living my dreams and my god given mission.

Two years ago, I couldn't even imagine this was where I'd be.
Today, I am continually grateful that I chose this, that I focused and created this, that I listened to my intuition.

I hope you take the chance on yourself and fulfill your dreams. Only you can make it happen.

Choose yourself and your dreams!

* * *

Everyone Gets Sad

Sometimes I get sad at what we are witnessing in the world today.

Sometimes I have no idea what I'm doing or why.

Sometimes I have to go sit in a room, meditate and cry my heart out (in no particular order).

The collective energy, the release of my own feelings, the attacks on the truth bearers, all of it.

It can make you feel that you've been used nonstop as a punching bag, and that's what dark forces want.

They want us to give up, to walk away or to deny our truth.
They want us to give up on our integrity, and knowing who we are and what we came here to do.

They don't want us to remember our power. Our gifts.
Our unlimited supply of love.

Many of us came here to go through extreme difficulties
and to rise up - to light the way for others. To be the
beacon of hope and love.

And we can always go inside of ourselves -> we can
always take our hands, press them onto our hearts,
breathe slowly and deeply and go within to the heartbeat.
The thumping that pulsates a bright light from within us
and around us, and is there for us even in our darkest
moments.

Because it was our choice to come here at this time.

We knew that we would walk through hell and laugh in
the face of the devil, and still continue beaming
light/love out of our bodies.

We will not falter.

We might stumble; we might hurt and cry and rage at
what is happening right now; we might need to
disconnect from others for a few days in order to come
back to our home/our center/ourselves.

But we stand unwaveringly in our truth. We walk daily in
our high energetic vibration knowing who we truly are.

We are sent from god.
We are the warriors, the oracles, the priests/priestesses,
and the muses; the kings and queens, the lovers and

creators. We are energy masters and apprentices, seekers and healers.

We are the ones who do not bow down to anything other than love.

We are here for our mission and we are here to create this new earth together.

We consciously choose - every. single. day. - to get up, be our true selves, go to 'war' against false light and false gods -> dismantling mind programs and hatred, and we continue loving every soul that comes our way.

There can be only one.

Seriously. There can be only one way forward.
And that is with love.

Not with fear, not with regret, not with living in the past or reliving traumas, or greed and denial. Not religion and guilt, shame and peer pressure. None of that is love.

It is the twisted version of a reality that is dying. We are killing it with unconditional love.

So remember - when you are feeling it all, when you are on your knees praying for light at the end of the tunnel, when you are sobbing your heart out to god source at the crimes against humanity taking place right now - remember that:

"You are loved and you are protected. You are guided and held. Ask for our help. We will assist you. We love you."- Your Guardians.

We are the rebels. We are the misfits. We are the weird ones. We are all of that and more.

We are divinely protected and called upon to fulfill our mission.
We are here for it all.

So rise up in your power - use your voice, speak your truth, utilize your free will, heal, create, and ascend.

There is only one you and only one me. But together, even if we are miles and countries apart, we are doing this.

We are living examples of love. We are receiving and transmitting the light and the truth.

We are what our ancestors prayed for to bring peace and harmony to this planet.

Say it loud and happily with me:
"I am here! I am free! I am love!"

* * *

When you keep telling/repeating negative stories ("this bad thing happened to me, my family, or my friend", "the world is so scary", etc.)
to friends, family, and acquaintances,

you keep bringing that negativity into your life.
Watch your words.

* * *

True Freedom
Freedom.
Either you have it, or you don't.
Either you create your reality, or you don't.

Either you're free to move around and travel where you want, or you cower in fear and listen to lies that keep you trapped in a false reality.

It's time to wake up.
Your freedom is created by you.

You are the magician here; the one who decides what is best for you, your body and health, and your relationships and life; the one who is guided by and faithfully connected to god source.

When you truly understand who you really are, what you came here to do, and that you will fulfill your mission no matter what, you become free.

The time is now.

The choice is, and always has been, yours.

But only you can decide…

We have been waiting for you.

Welcome to the truth.

***

You are responsible for your life…
You can either consciously create it or you can let it happen to you (by not changing/growing/moving).
The choice is yours.

***

<u>Happy Solstice!</u>
I, like so many others, have been releasing what is not meant to go with me into next year.

The ego deaths/dark nights of the soul/the questioning and seeking - these have not been in vain.

We have been asked to let go, to empty ourselves, to allow more energy to take the place of what we have released.

As we align ourselves even more to our highest selves, even more to our missions, even more to our truth, we have released everything we believed to be true. Everything that in our arrogance was not of god, which means of love. Everything that was expected.

Here are a few things that I have released. I hope this might help you or a loved one at this time:

- "It's not good enough" - this creeping thought that my book and my work will never be good enough -> from my childhood.
- All relationships that cannot go with me to my next level.
- Giving too much time/energy to helping people -> boundaries around my time with clients and others.

Clarity and discernment are needed.
Everything is moving quickly and if we truly say that we want certain things, then we must do what is needed for our highest good and the highest good of all.

I am using today to fast, meditate longer than usual, and open myself up to any guidance that I need. For my highest good.

I hope you do what is best for you today and remember how loved, protected, and guided you truly are.

* * *

Are you letting go of what no longer serves you
(what no longer deserves a place in your life)?
Are you emptying yourself out so that you can receive
(and have room to receive)
all of the amazing miracles from god source?

It is time to clear away the negative, draining and stagnant.
(This can mean people, jobs, houses, clothing, sickness, mental blocks, limiting beliefs, etc.)

Make way for the new, fantastic, and uplifting.
You are the creator of your life.
It's time to clean your house!

* * *

"It's called fear paralysis"
The fear of the unknown or not seeing "how" your
dreams will happen can stop you
from becoming who you came here to be.

Have faith, focus on the end goal
for the highest good of yourself and for all beings,
and trust in god source.

* * *

<u>The Victim</u>
If you say: "Life is unfair" or "That is unfair" or
"Why does this always happen to me?",
it means you live in victim consciousness and
are a reactor in your life.

Not an actor.

When something happens (a death, an ending of a relationship or job, health issues), see it as an opportunity to grow, not something to hold you down.

A death means a being is needed elsewhere and it is time for them to go where they are needed. Yes, take time to grieve them but also respect their soul by allowing them to move forward as well.

You are not entitled to a certain amount of time with any being. Appreciate what you had.

An ending of a relationship means both of you have grown as much as you could together and now it is time for the next chapter of growth (alone or, after healing, with another).

But also maybe you can now make that move to whatever city or country you always dreamed of living in...

An ending of a job means it's time to be introspective. What do you truly want to be doing with your life? How can you take the first step to do that? Investing in yourself and understanding your purpose is key. Health issues popping up - where have you ignored your childhood or adulthood trauma, stuffed emotions, held a "keep going" attitude when you needed rest, not expressing your boundaries and needs, running yourself into the ground to please others, etc. Your body will always get sick to get your attention.

We get these opportunities to grow and change direction but most people are stopped or trapped by them. They only see the bad or "unfair" side of a situation instead of doing the inner work and flipping their mindset.

Which kind of human are you - an actor or a reactor?

Are you creating your life or letting it happen to you?

* * *

Your complete faith in yourself
and god source supersedes any
guru, religion, famous person, or mentor/coach.

* * *

Jesus said, "Rather, the kingdom of god is spread out
over the earth, and people do not see it."
- Gospel of Thomas, 113

What are you seeing?
Are your eyes open?

You can see all of the negative (crime, hate, sadness, etc.)

Or you can choose to see all of the positive (love,
happiness, people helping each other, etc.)
and then you yourself become love.

This positive view is what creates the "kingdom of god"
aka "heaven" on earth.

* * *

Distraction (so as to scatter your energy)
keeps us from creating for the highest good and
living our mission from god source.

Focus.

When your energy stays focused on the end goal,
nothing/nobody can take you off your path.

* * *

"You are the company you keep."
If you know that your family/friends/coworkers are
toxic but you keep spending time with them
and getting embroiled in their drama,
what does this say about you?

* * *

Either you trust god source in ALL matters or you don't.
It's that simple.

Faith, love, expansion
or distrust, stagnation, and fear.

* * *

You WILL persevere.
Stay the course and don't settle.
It always gets hard right before the beauty and miracles
occur.
Deep breaths.

* * *

I'm 36 today.
But what is age and time besides a man-made construct
to limit and control something that is not as linear as our
brains suppose?

I realize now that due to the amount of healing and work I've done on myself, 36 is young.

In fact, my body and spirit feel younger and lighter than they ever have in previous years. I felt so heavy and drained in my 20's; my energy unfocused and spent injudiciously.

Yet now, each day I am getting younger, more joyful and radiant, as I continue opening up more and more to what god has in store for me.

I trust in god and know that I am protected and loved. I am blessed by the universe constantly and I take the blind leaps of faith I am asked to - without questioning or trying to reason my way out of them.

I wish the same for you, my friend, that you may have the love, grace, and guidance of god behind you for every day that you breathe and exist in this astonishing and extraordinary machine we call our body.

There is nothing more spectacular than the passage of another year that confirms your soul's expansion and your heart's calling; another year of building what you came here to create, to experience, and first and foremost, to love.

Our souls are not bound by time however this earthly experience is.

Use your time wisely, joyfully, and gratefully.

I send you love and happiness on this incredible May day, my birth day, and feel much gratitude for you as you walk this phenomenal, nurturing planet with me.

- Acacia

P.S. I started my day with a piñata birthday cake and coffee. I hope you start your day as fantastically!

* * *

Take some time today to imagine your life exactly as you want it to be.
Practice this every day for a few minutes for 14 days.
Use your imagination for good, not for worrying!

* * *

Your biggest growth comes from getting outside your comfort zone.
Doing that thing you're resisting the most.
Leaving that situation you should have left months or years ago.

* * *

Deciding you would rather be free than working the rest of your days as a slave to others.

Change requires belief.
Taking that leap of faith into the unknown, trusting that god source has you.

Only when we decide that we deserve our best life, our happiest state of being, living and speaking our truth, vibrating at our highest level, only then are we truly free.

Free to jump, free to get uncomfortable, free to shake off what is "normal" and step into liberating our soul to follow its path.

Free from guilt and shame,
we continue to grow so that we can live
in a state of true freedom.

How are you living right now?

* * *

Patience: When your mind screams at you to move out of fear of losing out but your soul says wait one more day.
So you wait.
Then miracles seamlessly occur.
That's patience, and absolute faith in god (source/universe/creator).

* * *

It's Time to Clean House
Under the energy from the moon (or on a full moon), take a look around you.

What in your house needs to go? Are your closets full of clothes you don't wear?

Do you have negative Nellies in your life causing your energy vibration to dip or do you doubt your purpose or dreams/goals after speaking with them?

Let's make way for new energy to come in by getting rid of three things.
Today.

Thank it/them for their help in your life and wish it well in its future home/future friends. Feel that gratitude for the ability to let it go.

Then donate it, trash it, or delete/block that person.

Woohooo!
Time for new.

* * *

Celebrate your small and large accomplishments. Every step gets you farther on your journey and closer to your goals/dreams!

* * *

"It's on YOU to get YOU where you want to be in life."
Just in case you believe that some magical unicorn is going to fly in and fix everything for you.

* * *

"Imagine better than the best you know."
- Neville Goddard

How are you creating your life?

* * *

Healing
It can take months or years to heal yourself.
Or it can take a matter of days, hours, or minutes.

The choice is yours.

It doesn't matter what someone told you, what your friends and family say, what everyone else is doing in society.

It matters what you say, what your soul guides you to do, and how quickly you want to move forward with your life.

We all have different options to heal - you can sit on a therapist's couch for years and never break an old pattern or toxic cycle.

You can pay a coach to guide you and they aren't the right coach for you (per your intuition), or they aren't a good coach in real life.

Or you can sit down, ask your spirit what or who you need to help you move forward, and listen to the answer.

The most important thing you can do for yourself in this lifetime is to heal your body (stored trauma), mind (old patterns), and soul (not living your purpose).

Then you don't pass your issues onto your kids or onto other important relationships. Then you don't attract toxic people into your life. Then your vibration stays high and keeps getting higher.

Because you keep growing, expanding and being the most awesome version of yourself possible.
And every day you evolve.

And every day gets better and better.

This is your journey.

Claim it!

* * *

<u>Choices</u>
Sometimes it's the small steps to the bigger goal.
They can feel as if you are making no progress until you see how far you have actually moved after a month or two have gone by.

And sometimes it's drastically large steps like leaving everything and everyone behind to embrace your true path and what your soul wants. Changing the situation to raise up your vibration.

Neither one seems easy at the time but looking back on it, you will thank yourself and have pride in choosing your soul over pleasing others.

How your life is right now is all on you - how you think, act, feel, and who you surround yourself with has been, and always will be, your choice.

* * *

<u>What are you choosing today?</u>
Take a few minutes every day to close your eyes,
take a few deep breaths,
and dream about the life you wish to create:
the places you want to go, the sand or grass under your feet, the joy of your freedom...

Our imagination is our most underutilized weapon of creation.
Imagine everything you are doing/seeing/tasting/hearing, feel yourself in the dream, feel how happy you are.

Do this for 30 days and watch your world evolve.

* * *

Fear is a lack of FAITH in god source and KNOWING that god has your highest good in mind
and wants you happy, healthy, and living your best life.

Stop the indoctrination.
REPROGRAM YOURSELF.

* * *

Don't give up.

Keep going.
It's starting to get really good.
I believe in you!

* * *

<u>You Get to Choose Your Path</u>
Nobody else.

Take responsibility for your choices, for your beliefs that have limited you and your dreams, for the life you have created.

Then take action.

Clear out toxic people bringing you down.
Decide you are concentrating on what you want instead of what others say is "possible".

Focus on positive steps forward instead of the past and mistakes, or bad relationships and unsatisfying jobs.

Only you can make your dreams happen.

And that starts with you choosing that your dreams will happen.

* * *

If you can dream it, you can create it!
For the highest good.

* * *

Reality

"For god has not given us a spirit of fear, but of power and of love and of a sound (calm) mind." – 2 Timothy 1:7

What you consume (fear mongering and divisive media, gossip, negativity) becomes you.

You create your life.

You can see evil everywhere and be full of fear. And think the world is "going to hell in a hand basket".

Or you can be full of love, own your god given gifts and power, and be at peace no matter the outer 'reality'.

To focus your energy on what you wish to live, be, and see.

To be real, loving, and healthy change instead of adding to the negative narrative of the current 'reality'.

You get to choose.

It's called free will.

* * *

Just have fun today :)
You are you and you are free!

My programmed default is being

super responsible and serious.
(I've got so many missions to accomplish, ffs!).

I continue to call in more joy and fun
until it becomes my true default.

* * *

<u>What is your truth?</u>
Unless you are willing to unlearn everything you think you "know", you will never be free to stand in your truth.

You are here to take your rightful place (next to god/source) and stand in the power of your truth.

But only you can take the steps to do that.

Only you can ask for help and guidance, for your part to be revealed, for the grace to walk and act out of love.

If you are unwilling to part ways with your past - your learned ways that have damaged your soul and your connection to sin (sin = not living in your truth and what your soul came here to do) - then your life will stay the same.

You will repeat the same cycles over and over again.
The same jobs, relationships, fears, traumas.

How willing are you to examine everything that has gotten you to this point in your life and say "it's time to try something new"?

* * *

You create your life!
Every experience is yours to create.

How are you using your imagination (visualizing)?
Are your thoughts positive (rewiring your brain)?

What are you creating?

* * *

Take a moment to be really proud of yourself every day.
For where you've come from,
how much you've healed, what you've accomplished –
You are amazing!

* * *

<u>Are You Consciously Creating Your Life?</u>
Conscious creation.
Either you choose it or you choose to deny that you
have the power to do it.

You can have joy and love and feel all of it.
Or you can reject it.

Your choice as a human is YOUR choice.
You can create your life or you can let your subconscious
create it.

Life is fun and happy and you really live (love, rejoice, cry, experience, feel every emotion); or it is painful and you are simply waiting to die.

Your thoughts are focused on all of the possibility and the positive.
Or you are focused on the "impossible" and negative.

Your negative cycles keep reappearing and toxic relationships consistently happen.
Or your gifts are revealed and you start living your truth; freedom, love, and joy. Following your soul and using your gifts.

You came here to live fully, not to eek your way until death, the miserly existence of the next day, week, year, party, drink, relationship, or drug.

What are you choosing?
What are you creating?
You get to decide.

* * *

You are the creator of your life
Consciously create it by using your focus, time, and energy.
You (and your life) are worth it

* * *

There are different techniques to create your life because we are all different.

Sometimes affirmations work.
Other times meditation, visualization, prayer, chanting,
or journaling.
Find yours, stay consistent, believe/trust, and
consciously create!

* * *

It's time to build your physical community.
No more isolation!
Call in your soul people, do something fun and
uncharacteristic for you in your location,
and connect to your tribe!

* * *

Don't forget to speak out what you want to create.
Yes, write it down and think it.
But spoken words are very powerful and
using your voice creates as well.

* * *

<u>Sound</u>

I watched a show last night about how sound is creation
- what came first sound or the creation of the universe?

They went on to say that ears/hearing canals (sound) are
the first parts formed on a baby.

Basically the show stated why sound is so important for
humans and that creating music/words that vibrate at
certain levels is what can connect us instantly back to

god source. (Think sound healing or listening to specific hertz frequency music…)

What you listen to is extremely important.

What you say (spell - ing, casting spells) is also important.
And from the time you are in your mother's womb until your death - vibration, words, and music play an integral role in your soul growth.

Many of us know this but as a reminder:
What are you listening to?
What are you saying to yourself and others?
What energy are you vibrating at?

* * *

Engage fully in using your imagination.

Dream about the life you desire –
daily for five minutes (feel, smell, taste, hear…)
Then listen to your inner guidance and take action.
You are the creator of your life.
For the highest good of all.

* * *

If you ask god for something,
it will be revealed to you.
But your vibration,
and who you surround yourself with,
can block it.

***

Do you complain about negative things in your life
(i.e. job, relationship, house, health, etc.)
or do you take action to change them?

God source can only help you if you take action to help
yourself, not from complaining.

***

The fear of the unknown
(or not seeing the "how" your dreams will happen)
can stop you from becoming who you came here to be.

Have faith,
focus on the end goal for the highest good of all,
and trust in god.

***

To-Do List for Conscious Creation

Write the answers down on this page, or in a separate journal specifically for manifesting.

1) What do you want to consciously create (manifest) this month? List three things.

_____

_____

_____

2) What do you want to consciously create for this year? List five things.

_____

_____

_____

3) What do you want to have created within three years? List seven-ten things.

_____

_____

_____

_____

_____

4) What intuitive actions are you taking for what you are manifesting for this month only?

_____

_____

Inspiration for Health and Body

Your body is your machine, your vessel, your way to exist on this planet. When you honor and love your body, you raise the vibration collectively.

Your health reflects what is going on inside of you, sometimes so deeply inside of you that you might need help in getting to the root of it and then healing it.

Your willingness to do what you need to do - for your health and body - means that you are saying to the universe, "I love myself and will do what it takes to put myself first! It starts with how I treat my own body."

Tell me one good/nice thing you are doing for your temple (your body) today.

* * *

If you don't trust someone, there is no point in having them in your energy (your life) or allowing them to have access to you.
#cleanupyourenergy

* * *

When you are wallowing in stagnant energy, you will feel aimless and lost. As if you can't move forward. Remember to pause, place your hand on your heart, breathe in deeply, and connect to your inner self. Connect to the now.

* * *

Disease (mental and physical) shows up in your body when you won't deal with your trauma.

* * *

If you need to be persuaded to do something healthy for your soul or your body, you might need to look at your low self-esteem, martyrdom/victimhood, and lack of self-love.

* * *

Are you listening to your body right now?

If it's telling you to rest, get more vitamins or eat healthier food, pay attention.
This is the one body you get and it knows what you need.

* * *

Disease (dis-ease) in your body is also from your conscious or unconscious choices that go against your soul's truth.
Are you paying attention?

* * *

We are cramming a lot of lifetimes (and lessons) into this one.
Listen to your body when it needs a rest or specific nourishment.

* * *

"Don't spend time with people that don't believe they are wonderful. If they don't think they are wonderful, they don't believe you are wonderful either..." - David Neagle

* * *

Ladies - practice some self-love (and great energy movement) by massaging your breasts every day with gratitude and intention. #goodmedicine

* * *

Your immune system is designed to heal itself.
But first you must give it a chance to do so.

This is why fasting cures and heals —
the body has time to repair with no food or drink to break down/expend energy on.

* * *

If you don't take a true day off, you will burn out.
#knowyourbody

* * *

Now is not the time to give up.
Take a break, recharge, ground yourself.
We need you, your gifts, and your light.

* * *

Have you ever tried fasting for one day?
Control over your body leads to control over your mind, instead of being controlled by urges to eat, sleep, worry, panic, etc.

* * *

Don't allow things you don't value to hang out in your energy.
Clean out your house of old items that don't bring you joy.

Clean out your relationships that bring you down.
Value your vibration!

* * *

Take rest as you need it.
The battle can rage outside of you but release emotions and attachments from within.
We are loved and protected.
For the highest good of all.
Keep going!

* * *

"Take back your power."
I see this a lot.
But what does it mean?

Stop judging.
Stop telling people what to do or what they should do.
Stop getting in other people's lives and business.

Start focusing on yourself.

What are you eating? Is it nourishing your body and brain? What are you drinking?
What are you doing for your emotional, spiritual, physical, and mental health? How are you healing yourself and getting rid of limiting beliefs, programs, and drama (trauma)?

Stop watching TV (mind control/programming) and stop thinking others know what's best for you.

Start listening to your inner guidance (intuition, soul, god) and following that ONLY.

Fear, insecurity, addictions, judgments - those are not of god.
Those are not taking your power back. That's giving your power away to people and taking no responsibility for handing it to them.

You are an adult. You are responsible for every single thing that you do, that you create, that you think, that you respond with.

YOU ARE RESPONSIBLE.

Either you take your power back or you give it away. Either you strengthen yourself or someone/thing feeds off your energy (power).

Every person or situation you allow into your life can give you energy, drain your energy, or be neutral. Only you get to decide what you allow.

Nobody else can take your power back for you. You have to decide that you want your power, that it is yours and yours alone, and that you are ready for your full power to return to you.
The time is now.
Rise up and claim your power.

* * *

"Take a look around you".

How many negative people or situations do you have in your life?
Move forward by clearing negativity.

* * *

How many days per week do you ALLOW yourself to really disconnect from your phone and social media?
To enjoy life in the moment?
To connect with nature or with new people?

* * *

Your body knows when it's time to leave a situation or a person.
Notice any fatigue, headaches, or anxiety/stress.
Trust these little nudges - it's time to move on!

* * *

<u>Burn Out is Real</u>
In relationships, jobs, entrepreneurship, and life.

When you are not living in the vibration your soul knows you should be in (energetic alignment to your divine blueprint).
When you stay in a living situation/relationship because it's comfortable and you don't want to hurt the other person.
When you are too scared of doing what you really want to do or being how you really want to be because you've been programmed to be a worker bee (work till you die yay!).

Playing it safe is easier than listening to your soul.

So your body sends you signs and clues: migraines, back problems, recurring health issues, mental health diagnosis, disease, etc. to wake you up.
But are you hearing what it's saying?
How many times does your physical health have to suffer before you pay attention to your body's needs and your soul's whispers?

* * *

If you haven't healed your mind, body, and soul from past conflict and trauma, you will keep repeating the same relationship and life patterns.
A drama trauma life versus a happy fulfilling life.

* * *

Take care of, respect, and love your meat suit (body) so that you can tap into unlimited energy and take action on the divine guidance you receive.

* * *

<u>How are you helping your body right now?</u>
Notice anything that drains your energy or makes you unhappy and stop doing it, being around it, or engaging with it. (This is also called enforcing boundaries.)

When energy is constantly leaking from you, you have less focus on your goals and the life you desire, thus less drive and less willpower to follow through.

We are in control of how much energy we give away. Tighten up your boundaries and your energy container, and help yourself flourish.

* * *

Monitoring what you consume
(media, food, social media, words from friends/family)
is one of the quickest ways to help you heal yourself,
clear anxiety and depression, and
control your mind and body.

* * *

<u>Nature for Your Health</u>
My connection with nature has deepened over the years. I ran away from my upbringing - running around barefoot on the Midwestern flat plains of Kansas - chasing city lights and a fast money-making life.

I took for granted the clear skies where I could count every star lying on my back in the grass, or see a storm coming from miles away.
I had witnessed the magic of nature in tornadoes and the largest lightning/thunder storms that shook my childhood brick home.

I have come back to my love of nature as an extension of love for myself after living in Bali.

Yesterday, hiking in the spontaneous rain and sunshine by a loch in Scotland, my soul began to run around like the barefoot child I was, seeing the magic and feeling the energies.

When was the last time you went out in nature, took a few deep belly breaths, and allowed yourself to be one with this beautiful earth we live on?

* * *

You can no longer operate out of fear, or dishonesty to your soul, at this time.
Your body will refuse to cooperate if you are living a lie.
Listen to your body and your intuition.
They guide you. Always.

* * *

<u>Your Body</u>
Listen. As a fellow human, I will fight for your right to choose what you do, don't do, or put or don't put into your body.
I may not agree with it or understand it, or even feel like fighting for it.

But I will always, 100% of the time, back you up in your RIGHT as a human being to OWN your body and make the choices that you think are best for it.
To live how you choose to live. To be free and have freewill, as we were made to be.

Because the only thing that you actually own on this planet is your body.
So treat it well and love it.

Only you can decide what is best for YOU. Only you can trust yourself for choosing what is best for your body.
Nobody else. Ever.
Keep being you!

* * *

We no longer live in the programming of "but it's my mom/dad/sibling/blood" excuse of why you MUST keep someone in your life.
Toxic is toxic.
Who you surround yourself with affects your energy and health.

* * *

<u>How Do You Speak To or About Yourself?</u>
Your body reflects your words.
Pay attention to how you speak about yourself.

Do you say things like, "I am stupid or fat or old" or "I can't do it" or "I have a bad heart, it runs in the family" or "I can't have a good relationship because bad ones are in my genes" or "I'm single because I don't need anybody and I'm a badass"?
Comments such as these train your body/mind that this is what you are.

If you can say to yourself, "I am beautiful or young or intelligent" or "I am fit and healthy" or "I break the generational curses and my body is healthy" or "I am open to a loving, god sourced relationship" for a minimum of 14 days straight, watch what happens.
Your body will respond to your words (your commands).

Your love for yourself will grow because you are giving yourself more love.
Thus, you will show others more love than you already do.
When we love ourselves - with our actions and words, thoughts and feelings - we change the world.
And this starts with being aware of how you talk to or about yourself, how you talk about others, and taking the small steps to create the new earth as a loving place.

As within, so without.
Love to you!

* * *

<u>Punishing Ourselves</u>
I used to control myself by losing weight.

This started in high school (14 years old) when I modeled and was told I was too fat or had too much weight on my hips, not enough jawline, not enough…the list went on and on.
So at the age 15, I learned to punish myself to get perfection.

I ate half a bagel or eight saltine crackers per day along with eight ounces of water. I ran on a treadmill for an hour or so in a water losing suit. I sat in the sauna to lose more weight.
I would eat meals and throw them up if I felt fat. I hid all of this from everyone and made jokes about people who did what I was doing to myself.

This went on until I went to college where I went the other way and gained weight to prove that I was normal. I ate what I wanted and drank even more.
This mindset continued in NYC until I would have breakdowns or feel bad about myself. Then I would get really skinny to feel better. To prove that I could still be a model. That I had something to offer.

I would punish myself to feel better. But at least I had some form of control. Because I was not living my truth and was striving to please others, I took it out on myself (my body).

Living in Bali, healing myself from traumas and emotional baggage and finding myself again, I did the same thing.
I couldn't control my business or my demanding coach, so I was punishing my body with rigid demands, fasting, and two-hour daily yoga.
I didn't realize how far I was pushing myself until I came back from Bali and my mom said, "You are so skinny, it looks bad."
And I thought, "What did I do to myself?"
I had returned to a cycle that I was comfortable with because I was used to pain and control.

From that point on, I made it a daily habit to tell my body how much I love it, how awesome it is and how grateful I am for all of the journeys we've been on together and that we will go on. I did a gentler yoga when my body needed it. I spent more time walking in nature.

And my body naturally started to blossom. To glow. To give me more booty and bigger breasts. To be and look healthy.
Not to look starved and deprived of nutrients.

I used to gloss over this part of my life. Gloss over the punishment I doled out to myself.
We are trained to see all of our flaws. We look in the mirror and hate ourselves.
(In modeling, that is even more pronounced because of the intense scrutiny.)

So we must un-train our minds on how we see ourselves, our bodies, and our souls.
We must re-train our minds to be grateful that we have our bodies, that we can walk or exercise, that we are healthy and alive, that we are human and we love our bodies.
Because loving your body is loving yourself.

I challenge you to love your body today.
All day today when you have a chance – tell it how grateful you are for it and the miracle that it is.
See how you feel.

See if your mindset changes once you start to love on your body.

* * *

Take a few deep breaths.
Feel into your body, feel your heart beat.
Breathe even slower.
Hug yourself tightly and say,
"I am here, I am free, and I am love."

* * *

Allow yourself to change your mind.
Who you were last month is not the same as today.
You've grown and expanded on a soul level and so have your thoughts and feelings.

* * *

Allow yourself to rest. The body knows, so don't underestimate your needs right now.

* * *

Pull your focus back on you, your mission, and your goals.
Protect your energy.
Listen to your intuition and then take action.

* * *

Beware the ego traps of superiority, i.e.: "I'm vegan so I am more enlightened."
"I'm further in my spiritual journey than them."
We are all different. We are all love.
We are all connected (back to god).

* * *

I hope you take time to listen to what your body and soul need today.

* * *

Allow yourself to be loved and supported.
Say out loud joyfully, "I allow myself to be loved and supported today.
Thank you, thank you, thank you!"
You are an amazing soul and I'm grateful for you!

* * *

Diet

I've been asked about my 'diet' quite a few times now.
So let me tell you why I fast.

First off, there are many different types of fasting. When I started fasting in Bali, it was with a three-day water fast. This was after eating clean, organic, and mainly vegetarian or vegan for many years.

Today, I do 'intermittent fasting' where I don't eat for 16-18 hours (the majority of those hours are overnight) and stop eating by 6pm.

Why 6pm? Because the pancreas goes to sleep at 7pm (a certain circadian rhythm) and doesn't process sugar, fats, or oils after that time -> they just sit there.

I give myself one-two days off per week unless there's an occasion (wedding, vacation, etc.), then it's four-five days off.

If I begin to feel weird or my body says I need to water, juice, or dry fast, I will fast.

I also do cleanses for my gallbladder and colon as directed by my body (My gallbladder was supposed to be removed in college per the doctors).

How am I able to listen to my body so clearly?

That first three day fast in Bali - I became so connected to every whisper of my body and organs that I could differentiate between it and my ego (that wants loads of food, sugar, coffee, etc. to slow me down).
My intention for that fast was to stop being controlled by my body. To stop feeding it unnecessarily. To stop getting 'hangry' when I didn't eat 'on time'.
To clear out my subconscious from old stories like 'but my blood sugar drops' or 'everyone in my family is like this'.

I enjoy pushing my body to its limits. I enjoy the clarity of my mind when I haven't eaten - when my body isn't constantly working to break down the food into nutrients and waste.

I know how important health is.
I refused to follow the three meals a day sickness plan.
I chose a different path that meant less food intake in a healthy way (versus my modeling days of starving myself).

Why?
Because I'm not out working in fields all day and burning 10,000 calories via physical labor. And I don't enjoy being at the gym for two hours a day either.
I don't have time for eating that much or working out that long.

I grew up in a family that valued no sugar or caffeine, training the body/working out (since I was seven years old -> don't even get me started on gyms, weight lifting, and protein shakes with raw eggs in them), and wholesome, homemade food.

I'm grateful for that upbringing and discipline. It helped me choose a different path a few years ago.

Yoga keeps me long and lean, my muscles stretched and firm.
Fasting keeps my organs and mind happy, and my body from excess weight.
I don't even like the term fasting. I don't feel deprived of food. I eat what I need and take vitamins if I feel like it.

I also am a foodie and enjoy a beautifully prepared meal in a restaurant (yes, I'm a Taurus too).
My blood pressure and health numbers are fantastic.

I think that eating two meals in six-eight hours is normal for me - one light, one heavy. It gives me the most energy. Sometimes, I only eat one meal if I feel dense or slow in my body.

I generally stay away from sugar and caffeine.
I get even more energy when I only drink my ph eight+ water for entire days.
And I connect more with the Divine.
Which is the most important reason for me.
My body is my antenna, my receptor.
I can only receive when I am clean internally and healthy.
I have willingly accepted this lifestyle to care for my body in order to channel and create directly with god.
This is my path to maintaining optimum output from my amazing machine, my body.

What's your path?

* * *

If doing something or being around a certain person drains you, do not do it or be around them.
This is energy harvesting & ties you back into the old programming of 'it has to be hard/difficult/a struggle'.
The new way (the new earth) is joy, love, peace, & freedom.

* * *

Beware the people saying there is only one right way -> one way to be in divine union, to clear trauma, to eat, to connect to god, to manifest, etc.

That's old programming.
Use Discernment.

* * *

Our bodies regenerate.
Aging is one of the biggest lies sold.
If you truly believe (mindset) that you get younger every year and feel better than last month, you will. Your DNA listens to your commands.

* * *

Pause.
Breathe.
Ground yourself.
Pull your focus back to yourself.
Direct your energy back to your mission.
You are right on time.

* * *

<u>Various Energy Stages</u>
Some of us are going through detox symptoms (for the healing of the feminine or masculine, collective, etc.) to release the addictions, the implants/entities, the programming; the deep ancestral wounds that end with you being born into your family line.
Some of us are sleeping a lot.
Some of us are energetically creating our best ideas ever.
Some of us are aligning with our divine union partners and co-creating.
The energy is different for everyone right now.

Allow yourself to truly feel, to release, to grieve, to scream, to move/exercise, to shift the energy.
Allow yourself to let go of your old self and beliefs, people or thoughts not aligned to your highest good.
Your highest good = the highest good for all.

Whatever you are feeling, remember to call on your guides/angels/galactic fam for help. To pray when you feel doubts or fears. To ask for help and support.

We are here. We love you.
Thank you for choosing this mission. Thank you for being you. Thank you for being.
"I am here, I am here, I am here!
I am free, I am free, I am free!
I am love, I am love, I am love!"

* * *

Hello, you beautiful soul
Whatever you are feeling, whatever you do today or this weekend, know that you are loved and you are right on time.
Breathe and connect with your heart.
We see you :)

* * *

If you want miraculous changes and to step onto your highest timeline, you have to release anything weighing you down. Anything that is the old you.

Are you willing to let go of the old to fly into your true freedom?

* * *

Nurture yourself right now.
Give yourself a hug and some extra love.
Take salt baths, ground barefoot in nature, move your body, sing.
You are transforming!

* * *

I had this discussion with a client the other day.

The reason why you block an ex or an old 'friend' or a family member who messages you and you want nothing to do with them because of different energy levels, disrespect, dishonesty, gaslighting…(messaging you = trying to hook you back into their energy using guilt, shame, people pleasing, reminding you of your past self, etc.).

It's a false story to say, "Oh, only love and light and have compassion and don't block them" because they need to see your growth and learn from you. That's your ego. They are better served by you blocking them so that they can truly move on. So they understand your boundaries are nonnegotiable. So that they cannot energy hook you into their lower vibration.

They deserve someone on their own vibe.

If you have grown past them, you cannot pull them up into your energy.
You can only serve by detaching completely and letting them find their way.
Without you.

You can't save anyone. You owe nobody anything. You are your own savior as they are their own savior.
Have mercy on them by letting them go and releasing the energy cords.

* * *

37 years ago, and around this time of day in a small Kansas town, I chose to make my appearance on earth. It's been one hell of a ride and it's only getting better! I went into the Akashic Records this morning (after my wonderful husband fed me fresh orange juice and a pink and purple birthday cake) because I had felt - what better way to embrace my new year than by taking a journey!

My intention before entering the records was set for any healing I needed at this time to further my highest timeline.

Once in, I greeted the guardians and asked for their help in my healing for my highest good.
They surrounded me and placed their hands about a foot above my womb while one said (telepathically), "We will begin with your womb as your place of creativity and creation, motherhood, and life. This will reverberate through to your heart and throat chakras - the opening and the expansion."

My womb was literally vibrating and being healed - to a level I never knew I needed. I will continue to process this for a few days, if not weeks, from now.

More was conveyed but the simple message for all of us was:
"Continue doing what brings you joy. It raises your vibration and keeps it high. There are no limits to what you can and will create."
Imagine, believe, create, and receive.
Thank you for being here. Thank you for all the love and blessings. Thank you for creating and being you!
I love you.

* * *

All that's been coming through for me the last few days is womb healing, womb creation, womb power, womb love.

How's your womb?
(Yes, even men have a womb chakra and are connected to their mother's womb.)
Divine creation -> purify the womb.

* * *

To-Do List for Health & Body

Write the answers down on this page, or in a separate journal specifically for manifesting.

1) What is your health like right now? How is your body today?

_____

_____

_____

2) What do you want to happen with your body and your health by next year?

_____

_____

_____

3) Sit down with yourself in a quiet place, breathe deeply three times into your belly. Feel your belly expand and feel your heartbeat pounding. Now ask yourself (your intuition), what does my body need to be healthy? What do I need to do to meet my goals of body and health?

_____

_____

_____

_____

_____

Inspiration for Internal Healing (the Inner Game)

Doing the inner work is not something to fear or get discouraged with.

Focusing on your internal healing and learning what helps your evolution allows you to embrace all aspects of yourself, your soul, your truth.

We all go through dark nights of the soul in order to expand into our next level, in order to create the life we truly desire to live.

Your internal healing manifests your outer world and that is why it is so important.

Healing those childhood and adulthood trauma wounds are your first step to having the power couple relationship (divine union) and true freedom (abundance, travel, lifestyle) that you desire.

* * *

<u>Are You Willing?</u>
Unless you are willing to unlearn everything you think you "know", you will never be free to stand in your truth.

You are here to take your rightful place (with god source) and stand in the power of your truth.

But only you can take the steps to do that.

Only you can ask for help and guidance, for your part to be revealed, for the grace to walk and act out of love.

If you are unwilling to part ways with your past - your learned ways that have damaged your soul and your connection to sin (not living in your truth and what your soul came here to do) - then your life will stay the same.

You will repeat the same cycles over and over again. The same jobs, relationships, fears, traumas.

How willing are you to examine everything that has gotten you to this point in your life and say "It's time to try something new?"

* * *

FREEDOM

Either you want it or you don't.
Either you want to be the highest version of yourself or you don't believe in yourself.

Can you do the hard and painful work in order to create the life you desire?
Are you willing to allow yourself to be truly free, in all ways, on this beautiful earth, at this time?

The freedom I experience now - mentally, emotionally, physically, spiritually - is something I work(ed) very hard at.

Something I kept digging at and going deeper into repressed trauma, my subconscious programming, my extreme distrust and disappointment in the masculine, my exasperation and anger at the feminine.

All of it.
That's what is necessary to become truly free, to open yourself up energetically for the future and life that you envision, that you feel, that you only dream of.

If you truly want to be free, to live where and how your soul desires, to liberate yourself from repeating cycles of the same unfulfilling relationships, disappointing jobs, horrible situations, sad experiences, and all that goes with the past, it's time to step up.

It's time to embrace the fact that you are responsible for your future and the life you are creating.

Nobody else is.

Invest in your healing, invest in your mindset reprogramming, invest in becoming the highest and best version of yourself.

Invest in your FREEDOM.

* * *

Doing the inner work requires hard work and commitment.
We feel stuck in our personal life and our business because we pretend or even deny that we don't need to work on this aspect.

We, our own selves, are the only ones who can free us from this mindset, to be able to grow, to flourish, and to be where we want to be in our relationship, in our business, & in our personal life.

* * *

We want to be enlightened, we want to be awakened. But most people refuse to do the trauma/shadow/inner work to get there.

* * *

<u>The father wound with a 'present' dad</u>
*trigger warning

Growing up, the majority of people in my small Kansas town thought my family was young, handsome, and happy; having two kids who performed well in sports and academia, and seemed picture perfect.

My parents were only 22 and 23 when they had me, the second kid; a daughter that my dad didn't want nor know what to do with, while my mom tried to keep the money coming in and the extended family from knowing how mentally and emotionally abused we all were by my dad.

I tried to prove myself worthy of his love over and over again by participating in every sport training with my brother and competing with my brother nonstop although he was three years older than I.

I couldn't understand why my dad never told me he loved me and why my straight A's in school meant nothing, or why he only would pay attention to my brother.
Why my dad was so self-absorbed and had no empathy for anyone or why he was the biggest hypocrite I knew.

But it didn't matter what I did, there was no affectionate love, no emotional connection or understanding, and even fewer physical hugs or help. Only rejection and abandonment - although at the time I had no idea what these meant or how they led to low self-confidence and low self-worth, etc.
I was on my own and solved my own problems from age ten, along with my first business and bank account.

Many times my brother and I were told we had only been born to be slaves, cleaning the house and taking care of the yard and garden, unable to play with friends or do anything fun until every single item was dusted, harvested, cleaned, and perfectly placed.

Christianity was shoved down our throats and our dad hid behind the 'angry God's will to threaten us, punish us, and make us behave.
"Spare the rod, spoil the child" was his mantra, so we strove to be as outwardly "good" as possible.

We were all scared sh*tless of my dad because he could snap at any moment; his temper was worse than the wrath of God.

My young insides screamed with rage, hurt, and anger. My inner child cried and begged the angry God to just kill me already. My dad had already threatened to kill me so why stick around sleeping for years with a knife under my pillow because I knew my dad would?

If my parents didn't want me then why was I here, I asked God every single day for 5+ years before I went off to college. Far away from my dad and his mind games.

And I spent years seeking love and validation from friends and relationships.

Until I healed my abandonment and neglect from my father wound.

After coming out of denial that "I didn't have it so bad" and "at least I had a roof over my head" as if I, as a child, owed my parents for being born.

I forgave my dad. I forgave my mom. I forgave myself.
I forgave God.
And I became lighter and freer.

This isn't the whole of the story, and many men and women have a similar childhood background.
'Present' parents but no emotions.

Misguided family loyalty and protecting the facade at all costs - even when that cost is to YOUR mental, physical, emotional, and spiritual well-being.

But once this wound is healed, once it has been brought to light and lovingly released, you STOP repeating the same relationship patterns (over-giving, codependency, pushing away, abusive partners, narcissistic partners, trying to heal/save your partners, etc.).

You become healthier and start attracting healthier people into your life.
Your energy vibration is higher.
You're able to create the life you truly desire.
You become free.
All because you healed a wound and did the inner work.
I've done the work, and I am a witness to the wonders it can do to your life.

This wound healing does not take years.

It takes the willingness to heal yourself and the readiness to release suppressed pain in order to live a happy life.

There is more to life than waking up lost, repeating the same routines and patterns, or just saying, "I'm going to be alone because it's easier" or "This is just how it is". Those words are not your truth. These are not YOU.

There is no shame in wanting more, in knowing deep down that you are meant to be doing something else or living another way.

But first, you must heal the old patterns and yourself instead of thinking you can handle it, you're tough, "what doesn't kill you makes you stronger", and all the other LIES we are told to say it is acceptable to have these unhealed wounds draining our energy and love and life.

The choices we make are our responsibility as adults, and the life we live is what we have created.
So ask yourself: are you ready for more?
More fun, more happiness, and more freedom?

* * *

Without connecting to our soul, without doing the inner work, our desired transformation, self-compassion, and acceptance will be difficult to achieve and sustain.

Which results in putting limiting-beliefs towards ourselves that hinder the progress and growth of our business/job, and our personal life.

* * *

Doubt and fear lead to chaos,
chaos leads to more doubt and fear.

How are you functioning?
Are you resolving and voicing issues?

Are you taking the time to see your trauma and shadows, acknowledge them, and love them as a part of you?

Or are you choosing the dead emotions - stuffing way?
The easy way? The "safe" way?
The way that leads to chaos and doubt and fear?
You get to choose the life you want. Your thoughts circulating in your brain and the words you speak out loud change the way your body and mind grow.

There's more to life than chaos and strife, unhappiness and perpetually searching for something better or a quick fix on solving your problems.

Take the time. Go inside yourself. See where you need some healing and some help.
And then take action on it.

Reach out to a mentor or healer you align with.
Ask your higher self if working with them is in your highest good.
Invest in healing yourself so that you can help those around you

* * *

Don't let your ego/inner critic slow you down in your journey.
Stop comparing yourself with others.
Your journey starts and ends with you.

It's time to start doing the inner work,
the soul work.

* * *

Are you paying attention to your soul's whisper?
Do you pay attention to its vital messages?
Like our body, our soul needs nurturing for us to be able to function to our highest standard.
This inner work is necessary for us to grow together with our life, our relationships, and our business.

* * *

Art/creativity – money/business – lovemaking/relationships…
If you're energetically blocked in one of those areas, you're physically attracting those blocks as well.

* * *

You can't expect change when you keep repeating the same patterns/routine that got you to this point.
Time for new energy!

* * *

Boundaries

If you don't have firm boundaries, you don't have a thriving business or relationship.

Most of us were not taught to have great boundaries. From our parents we learned codependency and people pleasing.

And this generational cycle continues into every area of your life until you decide to end it.

Doing the hard work takes effort and willpower. Not everyone is cut out for healing themselves and propelling forward in all areas of life.
Many will say they've done the work but won't invest in themselves, and still fight for approval from partners, kids, parents, bosses, friends, and even strangers.

The only person you should prove anything to is yourself. Only you are responsible for how healthy you, your life and your business are.

If your soul is weighed down under bad boundaries, a fledgling business, uneven relationships and more, you've got more work to do.

* * *

If you're "doing all this inner work to attract your ideal partner", you're missing the point.
#stopcodependency
#soulworkforyourself

* * *

How often have you resisted taking the hard action that made you uncomfortable or wanting to vomit?
In the resistance is where your biggest growth is.

* * *

Boundaries:
Never be afraid of putting them in place, for yourself, your relationships, and for your business.
Because it's HEALTHY and NECESSARY.

* * *

<u>Removing People</u>
Sometimes, toxic people who don't deal with their trauma must be cut out of your life.

It can be extremely painful yet it can lead to the growth you've needed.
Or if you don't cut them out, it can weigh you down like an anchor around your neck, dragging you back into the cesspool of reacting from your lower energy levels and ego.
Stay the course.

Your soul will say "No. That's enough." And you will listen and break the ties that hold you back.
Even if they are family or your one-time closest friend.

This new era does not leave a choice to keep moving small, to keep amongst those who aren't seeking their highest soul evolution.

Your soul is already moving forward. Don't let your human dictate the pace.
Keep rising.

* * *

<u>Stop Comparing Yourself to Others</u>
Focus on doing your inner work.
Cultivate your relationship with your intuition and the universe/source/god.
Greatness never comes from outside of us, always from within.
Are you surrendering to your divine feminine (intuition) or are you running around like a maniac in your low masculine (inner critic/ego) trying to prove something?

Allowing versus ego boosting.

* * *

We are constantly shifting and expanding.
Don't limit yourself by maintaining a routine you put in place months or years ago.

You have evolved. Be open to the new.

* * *

Your intuition only shows you your next step, not the entire picture.
If you saw the whole picture, you wouldn't go forward.
Move.

* * *

When was the last time you did something totally and completely for yourself?

Because you got so much joy out of it. Because it makes you feel like a child again. Because it connects you to your soul and thus, to every other living thing.

Do that again. Now.

Lying in the grass does that for me :)

* * *

If it scares you or you want to avoid it, walk or run right into it.
It has no power over you and on the other side of it is your growth.

* * *

Listen to your intuition.
When it tells you to take the day off and go frolic in nature, do it.

* * *

You Are Not Alone
No matter what your inner (critic) voice says.

Despite any isolation you might feel at this particular moment.

The journey isn't always easy, and sometimes we are tested beyond our limits.

But I've got you. And you've got you.

You have guides, guardian angels, ancestors, and soul family – all loving you and there for you to call on them.

Because we are all connected.

Even when you try to run.
Or pretend you have to do it all by yourself.

You don't.
Ask for help.

* * *

Hurry is fear.
When you rush, you create destructive energy
#flow

* * *

Let's stop emasculating our men.
They would love to provide for and protect us.
We must allow them to.

#ReprogramYourBrain

* * *

When was the last time you laughed until you cried?
It's important to experience joy and laughter.

* * *

Sometimes you have to say goodbye to everything
in order to move onto your next chapter.

It's okay to leave people and places behind as you
journey. This is your path. Nobody else's.

Be gentle with yourself as you move forward and keep
evolving. Not everyone will understand but that's the
beauty of growth.

Trust your intuition.
Much love,
A

* * *

Let's reframe the word mistake and instead call it a pivot,
a lesson or a test.
#positiveReprogram

* * *

What are you first thoughts upon waking?
These are the ones that matter.

#newmindset

* * *

When you repeat a limiting belief, it gets reflected right back to you.
#retrainyourbrain

* * *

"Stop trying to change the world since it is only the mirror" - Neville Goddard
#soulwork

* * *

Spring clean your relationships and watch your reality change.
#boundaries

* * *

Have compassion for your journey and how far you've come.
Lessons and tests help us grow and learn to try new things.

* * *

Keep the faith.
Stay the course.
Everything is right on time.
You are protected and loved.

* * *

You outgrow people, places, and possessions.

That is the beauty of life: limitless growth and expansion.

The key is to trust the nudges towards the growth and to truly let go.

* * *

"How you gonna win [love yourself, have abundance in everything, live your purpose and dreams] when you ain't right within [heal your trauma, retrain your subconscious, accept your soul purpose(s)]?" - Lauren Hill

We weren't taught to win growing up but we need to step up now - for the greatest good of all.

If you are being heavily triggered (tested) right now or feeling your body ask for rest, know that you are working through and releasing old beliefs and dropping more of your old self in order for your new human to rise.

Drop into your body, believe your soul's guidance, and embrace all that is coming your way.

It is time.
Allow, trust in god source, and receive.

* * *

Reminder:
You can say "no".
At any time.
With no explanation.

* * *

Using guilt and shame to get people
to do what you think is "right" is an ego trip
as well as emotional manipulation.
Instead of what they "should" do,
check your intentions.

* * *

DO you allow yourself
to change your mind?

* * *

Read the last line of what Jesus said. Wish I could highlight it...
Jesus said, "If your leaders say to you, 'Look, the (Father's) kingdom is in the sky,' then the birds of the sky will precede you. If they say to you, 'It is in the sea,' then the fish will precede you. Rather, the (Father's) kingdom is within you and it is outside you.

When you know yourselves, then you will be known, and you will understand that you are children of the living Father.
But if you do not know yourselves, then you live in poverty, and you are the poverty."

- Gospel of Thomas, 3

Do you know yourself?

P.S. The Gospel of Thomas was not allowed into the current day Bible by the Catholic Church. It has very mystical qualities and did not fit their rhetoric.

* * *

Asking god source for protection daily
gives the Divine the chance to remove/block anything
not serving your highest good.
True belief in god's protection =
there is nothing to fear or worry about.

* * *

The release of any grief, tears, and
bottled up emotions is crucial right now.
Let it out.
You are safe and you are loved.
Always.
Don't forget

* * *

<u>Help</u>
One of the biggest trauma patterns I had was never
asking for help.
I could handle it all - I could do everything.

I worked my nine-five, I helped/coached my friends and family through their constant issues, I volunteered, I fixed problems for others, I gave gave and gave.

Because I was taught to do that so that I didn't have to focus on myself (avoidance).

Didn't need to slow down and say to myself, "I'm deeply unhappy."

I could just keep going like a superwoman, supporting everyone else and never asking for help in return. Never asking for guidance or unconditional love. Pretending I was tough and I had everything under control.

Until I broke. After I had spent entire months and years depressed and anxious.

Then I would quit my job or leave/start an unfulfilling relationship or move to another apartment - a pattern I continued for 11 years.

Repeating a cycle of putting a band aid on it but never getting to the root issue.

Then when I quit my last "real" job, walked away from the only mentality I knew (worker bee), and turned my gaze within myself, I started to heal.

I healed the trauma.

I hired coaches to guide me after the trauma work because I didn't know what I was doing, or what my next step was, and I did not TRUST my internal guidance (intuition) yet.

Today, I am constantly growing and expanding myself in all areas - mind, body, and soul. Consistently surrounding myself with others on higher planes.

And I live a life full of love, beauty, grace, happiness, and abundance.

I know my path. I trust myself. I listen to my body and intuition.

I hire that next person to guide me as my inner guidance tells me to.

And I am so grateful I took that leap - that I left everything behind, healed myself, started over.

Because we get the opportunity to recreate our lives however many times we want.

There is no shame in wanting more, wanting better or different, wanting your happiness and unconditional love above all else.

You simply have to make the choice.
Choose yourself.

* * *

"As within, so without"
If you aren't healing your trauma, you're simply attracting more of it to you.
#traumadrama

* * *

<u>Spiritual Awakening</u>
Many of us went through a spiritual awakening as a result of a traumatic event in our lives.

Sometimes that was losing someone we loved more than ourselves, or maybe a death of a relationship or job we had built our entire lives around, or perhaps an extreme accident or physically hurtful event.

It took that traumatic moment for us to ask - "What am I doing here? There has to be more to life than this."

From the hardship of that period, we became seekers, searching for more and wanting more in our lives.

Not satisfied with the mundane existence most humans are marching into, quietly awaiting their deaths in attitudes of fear and despair.

You are searching for that sacred life of awesome awakening consciousness - that high vibrational, happy, grateful, god inspired life.

And this is how you fell into being on a spiritual journey, reawakening your soul bit by bit.
Coming home to yourself and the love within you.

You've got this.
You are protected and you are loved.
Keep going!

* * *

Focusing on others is a distraction and energy drain.
Pull that focus and energy back to yourself.
As within, so without.

* * *

Who and what are you allowing to have access to your energy (your time and thoughts)?
#springcleaning

* * *

<u>Are You Letting Guilt and Shame Run Your Life?</u>
Guilt and shame stop you from being who you came here to be.

They are the easiest ways to control people and break their spirit. They are low level forms of psychological warfare and manipulation.

You are not here to save everyone.
You are not here to be saved.

You are here to be free and to love.

Some souls chose to be here as teachers, some as healers of their lineage, some as grid workers, some as a wakeup call for others. Some as all of that.

Not everyone can escape guilt and shame -> especially when religions, families, and societies use it to control and manipulate on a daily basis.

Sometimes, the guilt and shame is from a past life or past incident that festers until it is unbearable and takes seasoned help to get rid of.

The first step to understanding these controlling manners is to see if you use them on others or on yourself.

Is your harsh inner critic dominating you via guilt or shame? For example: "You can't do that because what will people say" or "You should stay in this negative situation because you brought it upon yourself". Or "Why did you do that, what is wrong with you?" Are you then using this on others? "Oh you shouldn't do that because it's bad or others might think this…"

If you are using these, how can you love yourself and do better? How can you become the person you want to be?

If others are using guilt and shame on you, you must learn to distance yourself in order to free yourself. Stop allowing this in your life.

It's time for these negative ways to be cleared - cleared from you and thus, the collective.

That programming has been running long enough.

Guilt and shame are no longer acceptable.

It's time for love and kindness to reign.

The first step is healing ourselves.

You've got this, but don't forget to ask for help when you need it.

We are building the new earth together.

* * *

<u>It's Okay</u>
I am as guilty as anyone else of getting caught up with all of the things I should be doing instead of enjoying the moment.

I put a hard deadline on myself for publishing my first book by October 1 (which is not going to happen) and also I have two major life changes happening at the same time right now.

And last week I cracked.

I couldn't take the pressure I had placed on myself and I broke down crying multiple times - despite the yoga, despite the prayers, despite the meditation and walks.

And all I heard from my guides was, "Calm down. Everything is right on time. We have you. Enjoy your time right now because you will never be at this particular moment again. You will look back in six months and say wow!"

So if anyone else needs to hear it also.

It's okay.

It's okay to not do one million things at the same time because that's what you used to do. That's how you used to function and be known as superwoman/man.

It's okay to focus all of your energy on one thing at a time and make it phenomenal.

And have fun doing it - to truly enjoy it and put your whole heart into it.

We don't need to have it all together and remain calm nonstop. We are human. We have ups and downs. We laugh and cry. We need hugs and to vent.

So less pressure on yourself. More love and gentleness with your goals and your journey towards those goals.

Because everything is right on time.

You are taking the actions. You are doing your inner work.

But you are also living, loving, and being.

* * *

The energy is kicked up a level
What are you releasing today/this weekend?
What are you allowing?
Where do you need to tighten up your boundaries?

* * *

Reminder - there are no 'wrong' moves.
There are only moves made from love or moves made out of fear.
Ask your intuition if it serves your highest good.
Either way, you learn and expand.

* * *

Energy Leaks

Our biggest energy blocks and leaks are our relationships.

We ask for certain things and think we are ready, but we prove we are not by tolerating garbage in our relationships - love, work, family, and friend relationships.

God asks us to show we love ourselves by not allowing people to disrespect our time, our boundaries, and our energy, thus disrespecting us.

Yet we think we show that we love someone by allowing them to repeatedly do the same things. And usually they blame mental health issues, or that they are working on it, or that they need our help (manipulation) because they take no responsibility for their actions.

Enough is enough.

We are being asked to uphold our love for ourselves. To truly show others what total honoring of ourselves and our souls is. To be the beacon of love and respect so others can follow our actions.

That means no more allowing your family and friends to continue their behaviors; the boundaries have to be upheld; the people not on your future path must be removed.

Or you will stay in the loop. You will not get to your next level. You will not continue the journey back to love, back to source.

You would advise a friend, colleague, or family member not to put up with certain actions from any of their relationships.
So stop being a hypocrite and putting up with it yourself.

Actions are louder than words.

As within, so without -> your energy will reflect your actions.

* * *

Sometimes you have to get angry and upset in order to make a change.
Then you can refocus back on your breath, back on your energy and alignment.
Don't bypass your emotions.

* * *

Politics and Focus
I bet you don't know how political I used to be.
I thought I would go into local politics during the 11 years when I lived in NYC.

I lived and breathed my liberal 'values'. I volunteered on the first Bernie Sanders presidential campaign. I volunteered with indigenous organizations working with the UN.

I met people from around the world fighting for democracy and justice.

I marched with signs, went to rallies, screamed my opinions, argued with anyone who didn't think like me, signed petitions, and was brainwashed into believing that my vote counted.

I was righteous and I knew everything.

After the situations and people I witnessed via that presidential campaign and at the UN, I was forever done with politics.

I had come to realize politics was not real. It was a false god. A distraction from the truth.

Political outrage was being trapped in a false matrix - for if they can't get you trapped inside the religious matrix, they'll catch you in the political one.

Two (or more) sides of people pitted against each other instead of working together. Two sides of rage and hate. Two sides of "I'm right, you're wrong, the end."

Politics consumes your energy, destroying your focus.

Because if you're focused on politics and all of the division and how good and virtuous your side is, you don't need to focus on why you feel the need to be right in the first place.

You don't focus on yourself and your trauma that needs healed so you don't pass it down to your kids and others. You don't focus on taking back your energy and creating the life you desire.

You don't focus on being a living example of unconditional love and being detached with no expectations.

You don't focus on creating an earth where new systems are rising and people are working together for the highest good of all.

Instead, you focus on a political system, on a false matrix, that was designed to keep you burning with righteous indignation, arguing with everyone; designed to keep you fighting your fellow humans; designed to keep you in your ego/mind and not in your heart.

We don't have time for this anymore.
It's time to wake up.

Time to walk away from that false matrix.
To understand that your focus, your energy, your time, is better spent truly healing yourself and loving yourself, thus being able to spread that love to others. To focus on your true mission and your life and what you are creating.
Or you can keep fighting, keep struggling, keep wondering why nothing ever changes and it looks like it's 'getting worse every year'.

Break out of that cycle.
Open your eyes.
We are here, waiting for you.

* * *

A person who knows their true worth cannot be manipulated.
Energy never lies.
Stay the course.
Keep your focus!

* * *

You are right where you're supposed to be.
Stop comparing.

Remember who you are.
Keep going. Stay the course

* * *

Doing the Inner Work

When you truly do the past life work and the inner work (shadow integration, Hieros Gamos/sacred union, trauma, inner child, etc.), you heal your soul on all timelines.

Your soul is fragmented into different timelines. Time is not linear.

Your past lives and this life are all happening simultaneously.

Your highest self is guiding you (if you ask), and you experience the healing on all timelines.

Your Akashic records details your past lives and the gifts/powers you have had in all realms. You can access your earth Akashic records (or find a trusted guide/channeler) to re-download your powers (aka codes).

This will also speed up your timelines and help you heal yourself, your bloodline, and others quicker.

That's why it's important to discern the energy of those you want to hire to help you speed up your timelines (heal yourself).

Always ask your highest self if working with the person/guide is in your highest good.

Healing yourself helps raise the vibe.
As within, so without.
For the highest good of all.

* * *

<u>Surrender</u>
The hardest part for women who have been operating from their masculine is the allowing, the surrender.

Building and maintaining a business, taking care of your body, your space, your people, etc., plenty of structure and boundaries - all of this is easy in that masculine energy.

I remember how I poured all of my energy into my business because "you don't need a man; don't be needy, you're fine without a man; just carry on."
I remember feeling guilty for wanting my person to co-create with. Wanting to feel that support and love from my man.

I knew exactly what I didn't want in a man, but was afraid to be honest about what I really desired in my future physical union (marriage, kids, a family home, unconditional love, co-creation).

Then I would stop 'daydreaming' and get back to work, focusing everything into business and my inner work.

But as I healed my inner divine inner masculine and leaned more into what was oh so natural for me, what I had longed for in my bones - my divine feminine - I stopped struggling or feeling guilty.

I stopped hustling and running my feminine ragged.
I left my phone and business alone on the weekends.

I slowed down and I breathed deeply, unfurling the clenching in my sacral chakra/my womb.

I took the actions my intuition told me to - many were so beautifully feminine such as dancing, cooking, singing, and painting. And many actions were for my alignment such as energy healers and choosing particular clients.

I had to re-learn to be in my feminine energy; to love it, care for it, and embrace it.

See, I wasn't taught any of this.
I was taught that "being a feminine woman wasn't respected, only competition/being better than everyone else would get me noticed." I also couldn't trust or believe in any male figure around me growing up.
"I had to support myself and only I was going to do it - nobody could help or save me. Everybody would let me down. I could do everything anyways; I didn't need help."

All of my human relationships were disasters - I was either in fight or flight mode.

You can call these societal or family programming; wounding; trauma; limiting beliefs.

They are all the same -> a way to ensure that you don't heal your relationship with yourself, with your inner masculine and feminine, with the outer masculine and feminine, and with god source.

Because in the healing is when you begin to allow. To trust. To surrender to who you truly are, which is love; you know deep down what you desire and can have.

And when you align to that faith, when your energy expands with that true love of yourself, that is when miracles occur.
Miracles like divine union in the physical and magic babies despite an age.

That is when you understand your power and what you can create.
That is when you are a living example of love and thus, god.

* * *

True default modes of humans: happiness, joy, love, faith, fun, and gratitude
Programmed modes that can be internally dismantled (subconscious reprogramming): fear, hate, anger, scarcity/lack, self-doubt, and struggle.

* * *

In the search for enlightenment/ascension, don't forget that you are human too.
This world is beautiful, magical and abundant and you (your life) can reflect this.

* * *

The energetic shift is real, do you feel it?
Literally no fear.
Everything is right on time.
There is no rush.
The energy is vibrating higher.
Everyone is waking up.

For those feeling fear, anxiety, anger, hurt - know that you are loved and supported.

Know that whatever emotion you are feeling is the calling for change from inside you.

The people you once resonated with will no longer feel like home.

The politics or cliques or divisive practices no longer feel good.

You are being asked to choose your soul and your integrity, your dreams and unconditional love.

Choose healing yourself and releasing what no longer serves your soul:
be it your job/career/work, marriage and friendships, location, food choices, hobbies, addictions, etc.

You are growing. You are free. You are loved.

* * *

Be grateful for all of the experience you've gained
and how you are able to
re-align yourself to your highest good (highest timeline)
quicker now.
You're doing it!

* * *

<u>Passive Aggressiveness = Unhealed Trauma</u>
Please heal your trauma so that you don't pass it on to
your kids and to others around you.
Being sensitive (empath, intuitive, whatever you want to
call it), I protect myself from other people's energy
before I leave my house and when I come home - a habit
I've had for years.

I pick up on every energy and cycle. I can sense when
someone is holding deep unresolved pain.

The largest amount of passive aggressive behavior I had
witnessed was when I lived in NYC and it generally came
from people who I called friends.

When I chose to heal my trauma in Bali and not return
to live in NYC, I no longer resonated with these friends.
I held compassion for them as I knew what the passive
aggressiveness stemmed from (trauma).

But I could not be around them and I chose to remove myself.

Flash forward to living in Glasgow and understanding the culture here, and witnessing high levels of passive aggression.

Coming from people who don't understand the way my husband and I choose to live. To not be embroiled in their trauma drama. To instead look at life as full of love, wonder, and joy.

Because we have done the deep healing trauma work. We continue to do the work as we level up.

Which means not accepting passive aggressive behavior hidden behind false smiles. Fake niceties for no other reason than keeping the peace.
When you continue on your mission and stand in your integrity, it is not always easy. It is not a path many choose.
It means you have a very, very small circle.

And it also means that you will continue to trigger people.
They might not understand why you trigger them, but your very existence and even your smile and light heartedness makes them seethe.

They think that you have never been through what they have and don't take the time to learn your story.
They simply judge and release their frustration onto you (or try to).

And you, as a person who has empathy and compassion, as a person who prays for peace and unconditional love for everyone - you hold your energetic vibration.

You hold your integrity and your boundaries.

You release any hurt or disbelief that arises in your human body from their actions and energy, and transmute it to love. You know that you signed up to awaken others here (soul contracts) and you aren't everyone's cup of tea.

You remain at peace.
You are a living example of love and how to live in happiness and joy - to truly live in gratitude and faith. Day after day, month after month, year after year.

You know that the only change you are responsible for is the internal change - the change within you.

So you continue to do the work, you continue to pray and send love, and you continue on your mission. Keep going. I love you!

If you are feeling negative energies directed at you, you can say out loud the following:
"I do not consent to trauma drama/toxicity/passive aggressive behavior/etc. coming from this person. I do not consent to any entity attachments from them or anywhere else. I do not consent to any negativity. I protect my energy and place a protective globe around

my light body. Thank you, thank you, thank you. And so it is."

You will feel lighter (less sluggish or drained) immediately.

* * *

You know the way back to god source.
Deep within you, your soul knows.
Other people can guide/remind you, but the answers you seek are all within you.

* * *

I just went into the Akashic records and removed a deep ancestral wound from my line.

It was a circle that kept looping around me and my ancestors, making us repeat the same lessons.

I read the page where it began (the lack, the pain, the betrayal) and I rewrote it with love and compassion.

The crying release, the chest shaking emotional pain, the relief and the extreme gratitude…

This was my third time going into the records. This was an intentional removal on my end. This is self-taught as my soul has guided me to do. My guides were with me.
Remember how powerful you are.
Remember your gifts.

Heal yourself.
Heal your line.
It's your responsibility.

* * *

Internal Healing Practices
For any of you seekers out there, here are some of the healing practices
I used to heal myself from severe depression and anxiety (and become who I came here to be).

Please feel free to ask me about any of them and, as always, take what resonates with your soul

1. Childhood and Adulthood trauma clearing
2. Subconscious reprogramming
3. Energy healers for entity extractions and chakra clearing
4. Shadow integration (ongoing)
5. Feminine and masculine healing
6. Relationship healing and building with god source and intuition
7. Mindset change and word usage (affirmations and invocations)
8. Past life regression and timeline healing
9. Earth Ancestral line healing
10. Divine union (inner and outer)
11. Akashic records
12. Soul blueprint fragment reclamation

These practices (modalities) go along with:

daily journaling, keeping a gratitude journal, yoga (clearing chakras/energy), meditation (connection with source), breathwork (clearing), and conscious creation practices.

Every one of us is different. That's why there are thousands upon thousands of ways to journey in this lifetime.

I recommend finding a trusted healer or mentor (coach) who can guide you through rough patches -> someone who has actually experienced the ego deaths (dark nights of the soul) and healed themselves, someone who your higher self says is in your highest good, is a great place to start.

* * *

You are changing and evolving in ways you don't even know yet.
This is alchemy.
Allow yourself to go within, connect with your heart, and let it lead the way.
Balance will be restored.
Have faith. Stay the course.

* * *

Reminder: Your connection to
your inner wisdom (intuition, source, highest self)
is how you become a god/goddess (enlightened).
The power is within you.
Go within yourself.

Remember who you are.

* * *

<u>Entity Attachments</u>
People with unhealed trauma have no idea that entities work through them.

Did you think the "devil", the "dark side", the "negative beings", the "fallen angels" -> did you think those were all made up??

Unhealed people don't understand that they are being used for psychic attacks (thinking or speaking negatively about someone) to bring that person into a lower or negative vibration.

They don't understand that their words come from their own unhealed wounds.

They don't understand that their actions are used to make others feel as badly about themselves as they feel. They don't understand that they have no boundaries, or that they perpetuate negative behaviors in others -> by allowing them to repeatedly get away with certain disrespectful and manipulative deeds.

Stop feeding the addicts.
Stop feeding the entities.
Stop feeding the lower vibrations.

And heal yourself.

Truly acknowledge and understand your wounds - and your shadows.
Pull your energy back on yourself - back on what you need to fix in your life - instead of focusing on others.

For the love of yourself.
For the love of humanity.
For the love of creation.

For the highest good of all.

* * *

Reminder to call back your energy/power from every realm and any person or being you gave it to or left it with.

Do this multiple times a day, after using social media, and especially before you sleep.

* * *

Keeping a high vibration does not mean that you don't experience human emotions.
You are here to feel your emotions.
So feel them, experience them, and release them.

* * *

Stop comparing yourself. You have gifts you haven't even tapped into yet.

To-Do List for Internal Healing

Write the answers down on this page, or in a separate journal specifically for manifesting.

1) What do you feel shame or guilt about? How can you truly release these feelings and move forward?

_____

_____

_____

_____

2) What fears do you have deep inside of you? Once you write them out, you can acknowledge them and ask yourself how to release them.

_____

_____

_____

_____

_____

3) What/who is the biggest obstacle to you living your dream life? What steps can you take towards that life?

_____

_____

_____

Inspiration for Love

When humans speak about love, it is a term that gets thrown around a lot and casually.

Everyone wants to feel loved from external sources, but the main goal to focus on is re-loving ourselves. Truly loving who and what we are, at this point in our lives, now. Not tomorrow. To accept ourselves and understand where we are at, and to say that we deserve our own love first – that is one of the hardest lessons we go through as humans.

We were never taught to love ourselves and that needs to stop now. We are amazing beings who are full of love and we love who we are and what we are becoming.

Say it out loud with enthusiasm until you believe it: "I love myself and I will love myself even more tomorrow!"

Tell me: How have you loved yourself today?

* * *

Have the courage to follow your heart.
That's where freedom is.

* * *

When you pretend you are fine, that you don't need anyone, that you've got this
- it only gets you so far before you breakdown.

We need friendships and love.
It takes strength to ask for help or a hug.
I've asked complete strangers for hugs and every one of them has happily given me one.

This may sound strange but when you live in a country far away from your family, sometimes a hug is all you need.
And sometimes a hug is all that stranger needed too.
Human connection helps our journey.
Wherever you are at today,
I'm sending you an energetic hug.
I love you.

* * *

Don't spend so much time looking forward that you forget how far you've come. Love yourself and appreciate your achievements – big and small!

* * *

Do you know how to love yourself?
Do you love yourself the way YOU need to be loved?
Do you love yourself enough?

* * *

The journey to self-love is not easy because we are not taught it from childhood.
But once you love yourself completely, you realize that you are whole, beautiful, powerful and gifted, no matter what!

* * *

Good morning/afternoon/night!
What are three things you love about yourself or are grateful to yourself for?
Let's start this week off right!

* * *

Allow yourself time to sit in silence.
Breathe deeply.
Connect with your body and heart.
Allow yourself to BE.

* * *

You are loved and protected.
Everything is right on time.
Breathe.

I love you.

* * *

<u>Listening to Your Soul</u>
I spent over one year writing my first book.
My intuition told me on my yoga mat in Bali in early 2020 that I would write a book called "My Past Lives and How They Came Back to Haunt Me".

I started to receive visions and channeled the book in "streams of consciousness" writing for hours at a time. I did past life regressions and wrote from those recordings as well.

The hardest part was not in writing the book - it was in listening to my intuition.

Around the same time that I started writing, my ego started a business with a fellow entrepreneur (because business is my safety zone), and I listened to my ego along with a person that made an unpleasant business partner due to their own unresolved trauma.

I allowed my energy to be constantly drained by this entrepreneur until I woke up, cut all ties, and started over again in January 2021. This time, only listening to my guidance and god.

At first I struggled because I was used to my coaching business and serving others. Giving my artist's heart (for painting and writing) full freedom and exploration meant not focusing all of my energy on getting more clients. (I still currently coach a few souls who I know will do the hard work in order to live/follow their real soul blueprint journey and soulmate love…)

When I finished writing "My Past Lives" in May of 2021, I relaxed for a few weeks and then started the editing process. This cracked me open to a whole new level but I came to truly appreciate my perfectionist tendencies and attention to detail.

While my book was out getting edited (I even had resistance to clicking the send button!) by a professional, I looked back on what happened over that year of writing and who I had become.

And just in time for the full moon tonight, I am releasing even more of who I was programmed to be in my childhood and coming home to myself (and love/god/source) even more.

I hope that you are able to follow your inner guidance, come home to yourself and love yourself how you were born to be loved.

Much love,
Acacia

* * *

You are a human (with an ego/inner critic)
as well as a soul.
You came here to experience being human as well as to fulfill your soul purpose(s).

Be loving to yourself.
You are right on time.

* * *

<u>Devotion</u>
We are being asked right now to truly devote ourselves to love, which is god.

To not look at what is around us - divisiveness and forcing people to do things against their soul's wishes - but to look inside of ourselves.

To make sure that we are truly operating by and making every choice from love.

We are being asked to double down on what we truly believe and who we truly are - love.

Now is the time to step into what you, what your soul, came here to be.
Not just in theory or in words (with what you say) or thinking "Oh, wouldn't that be nice if we all lived in peace and love", but to truly act and live out of love.

As the struggle against free will and choice continues to be threatened, you are being asked to stand as god source has made you - as a pillar of strength and love. As a beacon of light in the darkness. As a safe haven for those seeking the truth.
And the truth is love.

Not fear, not death (because we will all die), not confusion or wanting everyone to think or act like you. Showing love despite the mundane annoyances, compassion for someone not on your wavelength, love for yourself, animals, humans, the land - all of it.

Only when you have moved beyond these old beliefs of fear and judgment, and steadily practiced being love - until it becomes truly who you are - only then can you create heaven on earth and live as god designed us; to live in and be love.

* * *

<u>Stop Hiding Your Love</u>
The love you hide within yourself is what the world needs to see.
Truly and unconditionally LOVE yourself first.
Then love others.
The rest will fall into place as you align with love and source (god).

Your soul purpose and mission(s) will help spread love throughout the world because of your true love for yourself.

Some days are harder than others but that is when you dig deep in your faith, take a few deep breaths, hug yourself, and remember that YOU ARE LOVE.
And love is what you came here to be as well...

I was going to do a live FB video today but we've had plumbers in, a real estate agent, random meetings, and all sorts of life happening on this gorgeous sunny day in Glasgow.

My ego started screaming at me that I should do a live and that I'll miss out and whatever else it was carrying on about.
I said thank you but I'll do the live tomorrow and for now, I'll enjoy some random stuff that threw my "set plans" of what I "had to accomplish today" right into the waste basket.

And I loved myself even harder for being okay with that and flowing with it.
I hope you are able to love yourself extra hard today!

* * *

There has been some intense energy lately.

Before you respond, breathe deeply.
Before you get critical of yourself, give yourself a hug.
Deep breaths and hugs = love.
Love is the only way forward.

* * *

I challenge you to do one kind thing
for a stranger today
(a smile, holding open a door, a compliment, etc.).
Spread love.

* * *

When you are creating and doing from joy and love,
you maintain a high energetic vibration that brings more
love, abundance, and creativity towards you.

* * *

<u>Silence</u>
Most people are so afraid of hearing their own thoughts
that they avoid silence.

"I like background noise."
"I don't like to feel alone."
"That's how I operate best."
These are excuses to avoid sitting in complete silence
with your own self.

Of listening to what your body tells you,
what your intuition (higher self) tells you, or what the
Divine is telling you.

The lack of true intimacy with our own selves leads to a
lack of true intimacy to god, and thus to a lack of real
intimacy with others.

Seeking out the silence, sitting in the uncomfortableness
of hearing/feeling everything you need to hear and feel,
and then knowing that within the silence lies every
answer you are seeking - this is where power lies as well.

Silence is a balm for your soul, an answer to your
prayers, and an exposure of truth. Where healing can
take place and anxiety/stress can ease up.

But we must be willing to sit in the silence and embrace it.

After all, we are all students of this life, and our journey began and will end in silence.

* * *

Three deep breaths.
In through the nose, out through the nose.
Send the breath deep into your belly.
Now smile. You are love.
I love you.

* * *

Say it with me:
Life is full of golden opportunities and I am grateful to see them everywhere!

* * *

I hope you take a moment to hug yourself and feel your love spread throughout your body.
You are amazing,
you beautiful, magnificent soul!

* * *

Enjoy the beauty of life.
Slow down. Take deep breaths.
Remember to hug yourself and tell yourself how much you are loved.

Because the truth is, we are here for such a short time.
And we run around like chickens with our heads cut off, forgetting to love ourselves.

When the simple act of truly loving yourself and acknowledging your humanness takes you one step in the right direction.

If all you can muster is gratitude or love, let it be towards yourself.

That energy will spread into your outer world and light up the beautiful beings around you, without you doing anything but loving yourself.
As within, so without.

* * *

Your relationship with god source is a direct reflection of how much you love yourself.

* * *

You are a divine being with limitless potential, energy, and power.

Stop letting your ego (subconscious, inner critic, and old patterns/habits)
control and limit you.

* * *

Don't forget that, deep down in your soul, you are LOVE.
Treat yourself (and other beings) accordingly.

* * *

Think of one thing you are truly grateful for.
Breathe deeply in while thanking that one thing.
Feel that gratitude spread throughout your body, into your fingers and toes.
Feel it expand your heart to bursting!
Carry this feeling with you today for as long as you can.

* * *

God source is PERFECT unconditional LOVE
Reprogram yourself:
Stop giving god human traits (angry at you, judging you, vengeful, etc.).

* * *

Some people had a rough weekend, others had a joyful one.
Whatever your soul released or made you let go of in the past few days, just know it is making room for the new energy that is coming to you.

You are loved, you are supported and you are free.
Don't be shy about reaching out for support when you need it or giving yourself a hug and a good cry.

I love you.

***

My prayer for you is that
you look inside of yourself today and
truly feel love for yourself
and then for others.

***

Monday thoughts:
Can you distinguish that which truly matters from that
which is a distraction?
That which shows you the path of love to that which
keeps you in fear and doubt?

***

Love yourself first.
Every bit of you is more breathtakingly wonderful than
you realize.

***

There is unlimited love and abundance everywhere!
It surrounds you.
Clear out your wounds and accept it all.

***

Don't forget to take a deep breath.
Deep breaths tell your body you love it :)

* * *

When was the last time you told yourself great job?
Do it. Now.
Even if you have only accomplished brushing your teeth today.
Love yourself.

* * *

<u>How You Choose to Live</u>

Most of us have distanced ourselves from people.

Family, friends, acquaintances have all been lovingly held at arm's length or completely cut off.

We have had to put firm boundaries in place and walk away from situations constantly.

Because the love energy we are protecting and holding is an energy that lights the way for others.

But the first step to it was loving ourselves in order to show others how to love themselves. To hold the space for ourselves first as we healed so that we could hold the space for others.

There was nobody showing us the way. There was usually nobody to lean on.
We had to learn the hard way. We had to go at it alone.
We were the black sheep, the misunderstood, the weird, the outcast, the ones who only wanted to show people

love but were giving it to people who could not understand.

And here we are.

In a time where the powers that are losing are trying to strangle the love out of people.

To divide. To make people believe they have no choice but to hate and be mean to each other due to opposing viewpoints which make us human.

To distract everyone from what can be found within, and what every human is actually here for: to love.

We come from love (god source). We are souls and we are here to light the way.

The way back to love. Back to truth. Back to what humans are.
Not all humans can function in community and love right now.

But most of us were born for that. We crave human interaction and touch. We respond best to love and hope; that's where humans thrive and create beauty.

Yet, we get to choose because we are human.

We can live separated, divided, hating, and in fear and panic.

Or

We can live in peace, love, harmony, and happiness -> creating a new world and working systems for all.

The choice is, and always has been, yours.

I hope you choose LOVE.

Every. Day.

* * *

<u>You Are the Antenna</u>
Think of yourself (your body/mind/energy field) as an antenna. You receive and transmit energy.

If you are eating bad food, not exercising, drinking booze, smoking chemicals/tar (cigarettes, e-cigs), pills/drugs, sugar and caffeine addiction, etc., what do you think this does for your transmitting/receiving?

Not only do these things lower your energetic vibration, they help keep you in loops -> bad relationships, bad jobs, bad situations, bad mindsets, and bad habits.

Now imagine that you want to only receive and give love, happiness, and gratitude. That those are the kind of experiences you want to have and give to others.

If your antenna is programmed to booze, junk food (not enough veggies and too much unprocessed food), pills, will you be able to only respond with love?

To flip negative thoughts to positive ones? To attract the joyful relationships and experiences you desire?

No.

You might fool yourself into thinking that "this is the best it can be" or that you are happy. And that might last for a few days, weeks, or months.

But then it all goes up in flames. You're unhappy and sad. You mask it with more booze/junk food/drugs/trauma bonding relationships.

And that cycle repeats itself until the end of your life.

Or

You can say enough of this. I am love. I came here to be love.

And I WILL do whatever it takes to transmit and receive love.
I AM!

* * *

My prayer for you today is that you practice more compassion for yourself
and have more compassion for others.
The world needs more compassion right now.

* * *

I want you to take a deep breath and think about where
you were last year at this time.
Then pat yourself on the back and say out loud,
"We have come so far. I'm grateful for you. I love you."
Because you have.
Keep going.

* * *

There's no overnight success in love, business, or life.
It takes weeks, months, & years of focus, persistence, &
dedication to your highest truth.
If you seek a quick fix, be prepared for being out of
alignment
with love and to settle in any or all of those areas.

* * *

Delete the programming that relationships are so hard
(hard work).
They are only hard when you don't truly know yourself,
you don't listen to your intuition,
and you don't know how to love or communicate with
yourself.
As within, so without.

* * *

Ask yourself if the food, situation, relationship,
community, etc. serves your highest good.
If it's a no, let go of it and move forward.

* * *

Maintain your boundaries.
If you don't respect them (by keeping them firm and not compromising them),
nobody else will - including family and friends.
#AsWithinSoWithout

* * *

Say it out loud with me:
"I am love. I align to my highest good.
I am in alignment with god."

All else falls away.
And so it is.

* * *

Not everyone is your friend.
Not everyone from your past can go with you into your future.
Learn to accept and release easily.
Discernment, detachment, and love.

* * *

Take a moment to sit down, place your hand on your heart and breathe deeply.
Connect back to your heart, back with love, back to god source.
You are love.

* * *

A bit of reflection about the past year is healthy.
Look at how far you've come.
Give yourself a big hug.
You are doing great!
Keep shining!

* * *

<u>Romance is Not Dead.</u>
Chivalry isn't either.
If you have a limited mindset, live in victimhood/martyrdom consciousness "Oh, woe is me!", or always think, "Why does this always happen to me?", YOU are the reason that you see or experience negativity.

This earth is magical.
The souls on earth at this time are beautiful.
Everything is possible.

Stop buying into limiting beliefs and repeating patterns/cycles.
Upgrade your life. Open your eyes. See and speak with your heart.
Only you can decide you are breaking out of the lies in order to live the life your soul has whispered is possible.
Only you can decide you want romance and unconditional love, chivalry, and your king/queen.

But it all starts within you. Your choices, your thoughts, your beliefs, your words.
It all begins with you.

* * *

I hope you take the time to connect with your heart,
focus on your future intuitively and feel into what comes
up that needs released.
Today is a beautiful, energetically charged day.
Do what you need to do for your soul.

* * *

Everyone has a different path.
Some people have to eat meat and dairy to ground;
others are purely vegan; others vegetarians.
Each soul is different.
No judgment.

* * *

Is your response to someone/thing coming from a place
of love, joy and freedom?
Or from a place of being right?

* * *

You are outgrowing your old community, people, and
places right now.
You are vibrating higher.
You are aligning with new people and new opportunities.
Let go of the old and embrace the new.
Give yourself love and grace.

* * *

The Word "God"

Up until around four years ago,
I had a hard time saying the word "god".

I had rebelled against it and only said "creator" or "universe".

The word god when I was growing up was used for fear, enforcing rules, and poverty programming -> something my soul couldn't take and warred against.

Instead of wholeheartedly accepting the Christianity shoved down my young childish throat, I looked around at all the hypocrisy, anti-feminine and anti-love that it generated and said "no".

And god was lumped into that no.

Because he was angry and vengeful and never answered my prayers. He hated women which meant he hated me.

So I spent years going the opposite way, hurting myself and widening the gap between myself and my soul.

Thus, widening the gap between myself and love (god).

When I left NYC after many mental breakdowns and my severe anxiety and severe depression diagnosis (despite all the yoga, meditation, and vegetarianism), I landed in Bali.
Where I began my trauma healing journey which led me to forgiving.

I forgave myself, my parents, my family, my society, and god source.

The truly forgiving myself was a big key - to unlocking and releasing every pent-up emotion I had stored since childhood.

When I was able to truly see myself, to really feel compassion and love for myself, my journey, all of the ups and downs -> I was able to feel god again.

I was able to communicate with the Divine and pray again; to share my dreams and aspirations, to share my doubts and to ask for help.

To build a relationship again.

Sometimes we aren't taught how to have a relationship with respect, honor, and love.
Sometimes we have never even witnessed an unconditional love relationship.
And it takes us time and patience to build up that relationship again.
To build up that trust.

Because as my relationship with god became stronger and more loving, so did my relationship with myself.

Thus, my relationships outside of myself - all of them -> they became more loving and beautiful, supportive and motivating.

Because as within, so without.

Which can be boiled down even further as we are all a reflection of god and are divine beings; we are all creating our reality; we are all unique and connected.

Speaking to the Divine daily, sometimes every few minutes or hours, and having conversations.
Really listening and feeling, and also laying down all of my thoughts and goals - it's the best relationship I've ever had!
When I say god now, I say it with love and gratitude. I say it as acknowledgment to the source that created all. I say it in joy and the feeling of coming home.

Because that is what your journey back to god is.
It's back to love.
Back to your true self.

It's going back home.

* * *

Intense energy for many right now.
Look into your own eyes in a mirror.
Place your hand on your heart.
Say out loud,
"I am free, I am free, I am free.
I am here, I am here, I am here.
I am love, I am love, I am love."
So it is.

* * *

What brings you pure, unfiltered, radiant joy?
Please take time to do that today.

***

Reminder: when you are surprised/frustrated because something didn't happen or fell through,
it means something better is on the way.
Feel angry/frustrated, then move on.
Keep your vibe high.
It's just a test to knock you off your path.

***

"We love you, we love you, we love you.
Slow down. Breathe deeply.
Feel your heart beat pumping energy throughout your entire being.
You are free, you are free, you are free."
- Your Spirit Guides

***

Say it out loud:
"I am a living example of love. My heart is open. I call in my divine union now.
I am ready now."

***

<u>To Trust Yourself</u>
When you do not trust yourself, you do not trust god.

You do not trust in "not making the same mistake again" or that you might let people into your life who do not deserve to be in your energy.

You have allowed fear to crowd your mind with unpleasant 'What ifs?'.

You have closed yourself off.
You have closed your heart.
You have run from your soul, your sovereignty.

Instead, you could flip the script and say I'm going to allow myself to trust.
Trust myself, and trust god.

I do believe. I do know. I do feel.

There are unlimited opportunities to tap into.
"I am a limitless being. I open my heart to receive the bounty of god, all of the love and abundance in the world. I am ready for my divine union. And so it is."

I say this as a person who used to prepare for the worst. Who used to be so afraid of getting hurt that I would use any excuse to run. Who didn't believe in myself or god.

And now I have complete faith and trust.

In god.
In myself.
In my divine union.

I didn't know this type of love or union was possible. I didn't know that it was all my choice -> to fulfill this union mission. To say "YES!" to it.

I readied myself to receive this divine love union.

I accepted the entirety of my being -> understanding that I am an ever-evolving soul in a human body, uncovering ancient rituals, and expanding in my consciousness every day.

My husband is not in this online spiritual world. He is not on social media a lot. He is focused on his mission. And what a freaking mission it is!

And I, I am here for all of it. I am supportive; I am his Oracle, his American viewpoint, his best friend, his wife.

I have chosen to trust in him at the same level as I trust in myself and god.
I have chosen to nurture our love, our home, his vision, my mission, and all that goes with that.
There are times where I have to find the balance. There are times his words are my fire and vice versa. There are times he comforts me and shows me what others see.

Because sometimes we get so caught up in what we are here to do that we forget.

We forget that we came here to live as and be humans - to feel, to trust, to love, to eat, and to co-create.

In all the seeking, all the communing with the divine, all the opening up to the old and new ways, all of it -> remember that it is all your choice.

Either to live as an example of love.
To trust yourself and god enough to allow for your highest good.
To do the work it takes to align with your divine union (inner and outer).

Or to fight against it. Against your soul. Against your mission(s).

The time is now.

Your inner divine union is needed
just as your outer divine union is.

The new earth requires your example of divine love.
It requires joy and freedom radiating from you -> so much so that the people seeing you can feel your pure love, your pure soul.

There is no bargaining. No way to stay half in and half out. No way to skip the ego deaths and the remembering.

Commit yourself to your truth, your mission, your soul.
Commit yourself to divine love.

And watch the fireworks; watch the miracles; watch the synchronicities; watch the divine union - watch it all show up.

For the highest good.
#hierosgamos

* * *

<u>Feeling the Energy</u>
It's been an energy moving few weeks!
For about four days in a row last week,
I vibrated on the current of pure love, joy, and abundance.

I have been able to hold that vibration before for three-four hours in one day, but never for four full consecutive days.

The week before last, I had felt a huge disconnect from my psychic gifts, which felt strange as this hadn't happened for a while. I felt exhausted and purged a lot of collective shame/guilt and war-fueled energy.

Over this past weekend, I did a land ceremony and healing within a beloved forest here in Scotland. The colors, the messages from Mother Earth, the inspiration from the trees - it was all so beautiful and comforting.

My husband and I did a lot of reflecting this weekend. We let go of a lot (material items and internal ones) and said a loving goodbye to our old selves.

We are embracing our highest timeline right now.
We are both accepting our shift into our highest selves.

We are both acknowledging how quickly everything is changing and how our ideas from a few months ago no longer serve us and our missions.

We both received blessings and gifts - materially, spiritually, and internally.

There is always a bit of chaos (discomfort, imbalance, etc.) - which then leads to the biggest growth for the highest good -> before the breakthrough.
The death and the rebirth.
The shedding of all that limits us; all that we allow.
The rising of the divine feminine and the divine masculine.

The glorious unfolding of you - in all of your beauty, joy, love, truth and freedom.
Abundance and love for all.
You are here, you are here, you are here!

* * *

If you wouldn't be friends with a person in real life, don't be 'friends' online.
Energy exchange is real.
Your energy is your currency.
Honor and respect it.

* * *

You are a living example of unconditional love.
This means you have boundaries.
You have self-love, self-respect, and integrity.

Keep shining.
You are needed.

* * *

If others 'judge' and criticize you without learning about you or why you speak your truth,
they don't deserve to have access to you
(your energy/your time or your social media).
Protect and value your energy.

* * *

"Just Vibe Higher."
I see people tell others this a lot, especially online.
Yet not everyone will choose to vibrate higher.
Not every soul will stick around for the New Earth.

And we have to be alright with letting them go on their path; not force them to stay in our energy -> to be around us as we start living a higher vibrational life because we must "show them" or "be a good example".

We also can have boundaries - of not allowing negativity into our energy. Or being in the midst of it in the physical world. Or allowing it on your Facebook page because that's your work/business.
It is spiritual bypassing to say "Oh, just vibrate higher and everyone else will too."
That means you don't deserve to have feelings. You should just vibrate higher!

I don't agree with that.

I believe in feeling what comes up, asking it where it's from and releasing it. Not pretending it didn't happen or doesn't exist.
We all chose the missions we are on.
We all came here with our gifts and chose specific families to be born into, etc.

But that does not mean that you allow yourself to be repeatedly kicked. That does not mean you make yourself a martyr or victim in order to "keep the peace" or "save them" or any other victimhood mentality phrase.

Do I know that the ascended masters like Yeshua (Jesus), Mary Magdalen, and Buddha did not protect their energy every day? Nope. I don't.
I don't know exactly what they did or what they had to do to fulfill their missions. Does anybody?

All I'm saying is that we are in a currently dense reality anchoring in a new lighter reality. The New Earth.

And sometimes that means you will get attacked for what you believe in or speak about. Apparently Yeshua and Mary Magdalene did. Not sure about Buddha as I haven't read too much about him.

All that matters is that we understand where people are coming from, let them go (unfollow or delete them on social media) as needed/if they no longer resonate, and continue fulfilling our missions.

We are all doing the best we can.
We are all learning as we go.
We are all remembering different aspects of our souls.

Those of us who chose the spiritual enlightenment path, we are choosing every day to vibrate higher and spread love, joy, freedom and also, experiencing the massive variety of human feelings.

But that does not mean human life isn't nuanced. That doesn't mean every human interaction is rainbows and kittens.

Yes, we are all in this together but some humans are not choosing the high vibrational path or the New Earth. And that's their free will.

As a side note: it took me years to undo the "never have emotions" wounds I had from childhood.
So when you tell someone to "just vibe higher" who has been in a traumatized place (which is 99.9% of humans on earth right now) and has only been able to speak their truth/use their voice for a few years (or months, or days, etc.), you are basically telling them to deny their own emotions; how they feel.

Or that protecting their energy out of love for themselves, self-love, (from those who do not want them to rise) is not an actual thing.

It's called gaslighting and that's not what is needed right now.
Truth is what's needed, not ego coddling.

Best wishes on your journey.

* * *

Taking the week off all social media, messaging, and my business.
Everyone needs to disconnect for an entire week – get back to basics.

I'm feeling the call to recalibrate and ground.

Listen to your intuition, follow your soul, refocus on yourself and place your energy on your mission and your inner world.
You've got this!
Stay the course.
Keep the faith.
You are love and you are here!

* * *

What makes you truly feel happy?
Do more of that/those things and feel the joy,
feel the freedom, feel your soul
For the highest good of you,
for the highest good of all!

* * *

Dear Divine Feminine,
Your Divine Masculine requires your complete loyalty, faith, vulnerability, and love.

He will energetically feel if you have these within
yourself (for yourself) and come towards you.

If he does not feel those values within you,
he is repelled.

* * *

Remember: Your Divine Union counterpart shows up as
an energetic match for you.
If you still don't trust men/women, or know you need to
heal more, do your inner work.
Then watch the magic happen!
#aswithinsowithout

* * *

A person's truth is found within them,
not from another person or outside of them.
As within, so without.

* * *

There is not only one way back to god source or love,
just as there is not only one way to be human,
or one country to live in,
or one way to be love.

Every person has their own journey.

* * *

Dancing, singing, walking in nature,
fulfilling your mission/your passion ->
whatever gives you joy and drops you into the
present moment
increases your light quotient
(the amount of light/energy you can hold).
Keep shining

* * *

To-Do List for Love

Write the answers down on this page, or in a separate journal specifically for manifesting.

1) What do you actually believe about love? What do you really (in your depths) feel towards men/women?

   _____

   _____

   _____

2) What do you truly desire for your love life? Ask your soul/heart (intuition) this.

   _____

   _____

   _____

3) Do you love yourself enough to change your belief of love? Will you show yourself the love that you want to receive from another (your person)? How can you show yourself this love *(list action steps below)*?

_____

_____

_____

_____

_____

_____

Inspiration for Soul Mission / Purpose

Your soul mission or purpose is unique to you! You are here to live, love, laugh, and play and create the type of planet that you truly want to live on.

And this means that there is something deep inside of you that wants to come out and play – that wants you to acknowledge that it is a part of what you came here to do.

Now, this is different for everyone. But the first place to start is to sit down in a quiet place, and go back into your childhood and think about what you LOVED to do. What you were drawn to. And ask yourself, if you could do anything right now, what would that be?

Your dreams are a part of your soul mission. Are you willing to take the chance on yourself to fulfill your dreams?

How comfortable are you with
surrendering to the highest good, trusting 100% that you
will achieve your mission,
and allowing god source to work without you forcing
your will/ego?

* * *

Most of us were taught when we were children that "you
can't make money doing what you love".
You should study and work hard to land your dream job,
a real job they said.
But this new era is teaching us the opposite way.
Do what you love, be passionate about it, make money
out of it.
This new era lets us discover the deeper personality that
we have, our fullest authentic self, ready to explore and
engage in limitless possibilities!

* * *

<u>To All of You Weirdos and Black Sheep</u>
You are a beacon - shining and multiplying your light
every day.

Even when you get disheartened, even when you get a
bit scared, when you feel that your back is to the wall,
you dig down deep inside yourself and have faith that
you are on YOUR path.

That you are living your purpose by being love and
spreading truth.

Others look to you for guidance - for the gentle voice of god through you, for the shelter in the storm, for the love you willingly transmit.

They might not say anything. They might never comment or like or message.
But you give them hope.
You give them courage.

You show them that there is a different way to live, to be, to come back to their soul time and time again.

Don't forget how much light you spread by simply being you. By using your gifts which shows others that they can do the same. By loving yourself, by honoring your soul no matter what.

You are the truth.
You are the love.
Keep going.

Sending you my love.
Happy weekend, my beautiful, amazing, soul inspiring friends!

* * *

<u>Keep Expanding</u>
Don't let your ego (brain, human) convince you that you are more knowledgeable, spiritual, or higher vibe than everyone else.
That everyone should listen to you or learn from you.

Yes, many of us know and have experienced a lot and that's why we are where we are, helping others to go back to their souls and their truth.

But there is always more to uncover, more to learn, more to love, more talents in ourselves to discover.

Don't limit what you learn, or how you grow, or where a path might take you - just because you think you know it all already.

Listen to the old guy telling you about his story, the old woman next door who doesn't have anyone else to talk to, the child with huge eyes telling you their crazy secret or about their visits with the fairies.

There is only one person limiting your expansion.
You.

Be open to the possibility of learning more.
YOU are worth it.

* * *

<u>There Can Be Only One</u>
There can be only ONE.
One you, that is.

Don't forget how powerful you are.
Don't forget you are creating your reality.
Don't forget that you can heal yourself of anything.

Stop searching outside of yourself and look within.

You are here, right now, at this time on earth, because you chose to light a path for people.

You get to choose to use your gifts for the highest good of all. Or not.

You get to choose to deny and ignore your gifts. Or not.

Whatever you decide, whatever path you take -> this is your choice.
Your free will. Your responsibility.

Nobody else can make your decisions or live your life for you.
So decide.

"What life am I creating for myself? Is this who I want to be? Are these my true dreams and gifts? I'm ready to do what I came here to do."

Or

"I'm staying stuck because it's comfortable. I'm doing what others think I should. I'm miserable and know something is missing. But oh well what can I do?"

And simply know, when you look back in many many years and say "I chose this path", that this has all been your choice.

It's all on YOU.

* * *

Your power is stronger than anything that goes against you.
Either you take back your power or you give it away.
The choice is yours.

* * *

Doubt and fear weakens the human spirit, which in turn produces more doubt and fear.

If you can't distinguish between what brings you doubt/fear and what gives you joy/love, it's time to start learning.

* * *

Reminder: you don't owe anyone a response or an explanation.
Anytime you react/respond, you exchange energy.
Guard your energy.
You cannot 'enlighten' people to your energy level, your soul mission/vision or your love.

* * *

Put yourself first.
Stop running around taking care of everyone else before yourself.

What do you dream? What do YOU desire?

How can you live your dreams if you are focusing your energy on everyone else?

Refocus on you. Refocus on what you want to achieve, create, innovate, and bring to life.
It's time to be who you truly are meant to be.

* * *

Let's talk about how you've stopped yourself from living life at 100%.

You've settled for less - in relationships, business, money, sex, love, art, soul creation...

This list goes on. But it doesn't have to.

You are ready to welcome more into your life.
More creativity, more love, more money, more happiness, MORE FREEDOM.

What it boils down to is being willing.
Willing to do the work to live this amazing life you dream of.

Willing to cut out the toxic people and thoughts, and to leave the old way of doing things in the dust behind you.

The journey to more starts by accepting your dreams, your god given mission, your gifts and talents, and screaming, "YES! I ACCEPT!"
Are you ready to become the queen or king you are meant to be?

Are you ready to lead the way for others, to live as an example of how life can truly be lived at 100%?

If the whispers from your soul are drowning out your logical brain and you're ready for FREEDOM and JOY, then move!

Take a chance on YOU!

* * *

<u>The New Era</u>
I always was taken with the idea of being a Renaissance woman.
They only said this about men back in the day; but the idea of developing my brain and hobbies to my full capability intrigued me from age eight.

As children, most of us were taught we had to get a job, make money, provide for our families, buy a house, etc.

We weren't taught that you can make money doing what you love, or how to have multiple streams of income from all of your passions.

When we think in this limitless way, and most of our passions overlap and birth new projects, innovations, and interests, we begin to truly tap into our souls.

Yet to truly become the fullest, authentic being we have the power to become isn't an easy road.

Many people say you can't or shouldn't or it's not responsible. The same excuses they used to stay small.

But we don't listen. We keep growing and changing, laughing and loving ourselves to the point where we stand in our full divine power and are untouched by the low vibes trying to pull us back down to their level.

We have received our gifts and talents from god source; our interests and passions are the spark that draws people to us and sets our soul on fire.

Most of us seem so different, yet we are so similar deep down.

Delve into your soul, your talents, the whispers from your intuition and the signs from god. Rise up into your power, become your true Renaissance self.

The self with many passions, many specialties, and so much love to give and receive that nothing stops you.

And nothing can put you off your course, for it is divinely led, and only you have answered the call.

* * *

You get to choose: your soul's purpose or your mind's way of doing things.
Love versus fear,
limitless versus limiting.

* * *

The Old Way versus The New Way

For years, I lived as the quintessential independent woman;
proving myself in a patriarchal society to the detriment of my soul.

I had to hustle, showcase my intelligence nonstop, get shut down by male bosses, lose my Midwestern accent or get laughed at, and not wear anything too sexy or be too threatening (smart) in a meeting.

This entire deletion of the feminine from my being brought about narcissistic and/or codependent men in my relationships, along with my own lack of confidence and self-worth that led me to be narcissistic or codependent.

But it doesn't have to be this way.
Women - we aren't made to be masculine.
There is a reason we are different.
A reason we are soft and giving, loving and free.

We don't have to hate men or prove we are better than them. Men want to step up and show us how they can provide for and protect us - emotionally, physically, mentally, and spiritually.

In turn, we must allow. Not say we know better or we are the smartest. We must accept. Not get defensive or say I can do it myself.

We must start healing this relationship with the masculine in order to become our full radiant feminine. Which is what you really want to be, deep down in your soul.

It's time to do the work.

Go into the hard places, delete the "feminist" programming and hatred or emasculation of men, and really embrace who you truly are.

Shine into your divine feminine and magnetize the masculine to provide for you in every area of your life.
Men - it's time to step up.
Stop being emasculated by rules that don't speak to your soul, by women who belittle you and criticize, by friends who don't see your worth and compete with you.

It's time to rise up and claim your throne.

To offer unconditional love and admiration to your woman. To have that devotion from the feminine that you long for, the true partnership of divine union.
This healing requires diligence and commitment. Not excuses and saying maybe next month.

The new era is now. The new energy to live how you want to live and love is alive and kicking now.

If you are ready to live in your full glory, to unleash your soul, to create the love and life you desire, take the intuitive nudges to fulfill your mission.

Do the inner work, hire a coach or therapist, join that shadow work group on Facebook.

Just take the first step and watch the rest unfold due to your actions….

* * *

We are here to live out our soul's purpose in this body. Get your mind and body on optimum output to fulfill your mission.
You've got this.

* * *

We are here to evolve and help others evolve. Stop trying to control everything and stop making excuses as to why you're in the same situation/pattern/etc.
Your growth is required.

* * *

Keep expanding and sharing your truth.
We love to see you shine!

* * *

Burn (delete) the desire to do 'what you're supposed to do' / what looks or sounds good.

Run towards the opportunity that doesn't make sense but is what your intuition said to do.

That's where the gold is (for every aspect of your life).

* * *

If you keep waiting (procrastinating),
it will never be the "right" time.

* * *

Nobody else can sing your song or write your story.
Live your dreams.

* * *

Your purpose or mission (why you are here) is what
YOU say it is.
Not what your family, friends, or society says.
YOU.

* * *

Knowing what your soul truly wants (not what your ego
wants) is where your power lies.
#introspection

* * *

The Fears

I'm not going to lie…this past week I dealt with some nasty fears that wanted me to stay small.

They kept saying "stay where it's comfortable, stay on this level, you know your surroundings here."

I replied NO. I'm sick of this. Time for change; time for the uplevel.

I turned 35. I dyed my hair blonde (something I would never contemplate before). I swam in a freezing waterfall.

I laughed my face off.

I said YES! to everything that came my way last week. No contemplation of if I should or not.

And this is how the inner journey sweeps you up into who you are meant to be.

If you are not working on yourself (because your surroundings are a reflection of your inner work) constantly, then what are you doing?

You're killing your soul. Telling your TRUE self that you can't be the star you want to be, the voice for millions, the bestselling author, the TEDx speaker, the artist extraordinaire, the incredible entrepreneur.

Why are you wasting your time, letting your ego tell you where to go and how big you will get?

This is the four hour workday era. This is the divine love and a sacred union era. This is the conscious, awake artist and entrepreneurs era.

We are the voices who will be heard and splashed across the media. We are the thought leaders and innovators who are unstoppable.

Now is the time to embrace the unknown, to feel your soul telling you exactly what it wants, to know in your bones that THIS is what you are meant to do and you won't stop. EVER.

Are you ready?

* * *

Tell me one of your biggest dreams
(for life, business, health, anything).
Say it out loud. Strong, proud, happy, excited, and joyful!

* * *

You are needed to share your gifts with the world.
Stop hiding!

* * *

What's stopping you?
Hold up...stop pretending anything or anyone is preventing you from living.
You are preventing yourself from truly living by not living from your truth, your heart, and your soul.

* * *

When was the last time you were excited to wake up in the morning (besides the weekend)?

When you are living your soul purpose, you naturally wake up excited and ready for all of the opportunities coming your way!

* * *

Focus.
Where is your energy leaking?
What are you allowing to distract you (your energy) from achieving your mission (goals)?

* * *

<u>Compassion is Needed Right Now</u>
For yourself and others.

Everyone is on a different journey, ascending at different times and in different ways than you.
Letting go and detaching is hard for the majority of people.

Living in fear and panic cultivated nonstop by society and the media is at an all-time high today. The spiritual and psychological warfare on the masses is not a joke.

Living in love, joy, and compassion is an intentional choice. Every. Day.
We are the light. We are the love.
We are doing god's work.

We have fought these battles (inner and outer) before. In other lifetimes. On other planets. And we win. Every. Single. Time.

Don't forget who you are and why you are here.
Love wins. The Divine wins.

* * *

Allowing yourself to change your mind is a powerful lesson in growth and expansion.
Have the faith in yourself to change your mind.

* * *

If you consider investing in yourself
(i.e. your internal growth/healing, your health, or building your own business/doing your dream work)
a risk that you aren't prepared to take,
you don't value yourself.

* * *

"Just Keep Busy"
One habit that is hard to break is the constant "staying busy" mentality.

If you come from the corporate world or a dysfunctional/toxic home life, safety is felt in staying busy and being preoccupied.

Then you don't have to sit in silence and listen to your guidance. Then you can ignore warning signs and red flags. Then you can pretend everything is fine and that you are in control.

But when you can truly break the busy-ness habit and sit in the stillness, and really ask your inner self all of the questions that you have:
"Who am I really - apart from a parent, sibling, entrepreneur, employee, etc.?
What am I here on earth to do?",
that is when you start to understand.

You came here with a mission. You came here with gifts that are unique to your soul blueprint.

You did not come here to be a cog in the wheel, a brick in the wall, a fearful shell of a human being staying busy with meaningless tasks until you die, a human being who is afraid of the silence.

So the question remains:
Who are you?

* * *

We signed up for this.
We are anchored in god's love and truth.
Stay the course.
(And protect your energy diligently right now.)

* * *

<u>Our Path</u>
Sometimes we do not know our path.
We do not understand why god sent us here at this time.

We cannot see it clearly or we feel that years have been wasted with so many bad decisions (lessons).

Our path is buried under layers of guilt, shame, doubt, and fear; trauma and societal programming; New Age spirituality and false gods - "love and light" even as all hell is breaking loose.

And in the darkest moments or when the levee breaks and the tears won't stop, when there seems to be no way home, no clear path back to love - that is when we have witnessed, time and time again, that we have come here to fight the fires. To wage the battles. To open ourselves up to what we came here to do. To do god's mission.

That mission is love and a new earth system created in love, because god is love.

That mission is not simple because it's easier to react or respond in anger, aggression, fear and pain. To get dragged into the politics/media matrix or scarcity mindset. But those are not of god. That is not the plan for earth.
God is protecting you and guiding you. You have been unseen or unknown because it was not time yet.

You are here because you agreed to this mission. You are here because you are powerful and have unlimited gifts waiting for you to tap into them.

You are here because it is time.
The time is now.
Rise up.

***

Seal up your energy.
Release what needs to go.
Embrace your truth.
There's powerful energy right now and your next chapter is unfolding.
It's time to rise.

***

<u>"Sin"</u>
Let me redefine sin here.

"Know thyself."
Sin is something we produce within ourselves when we forget who we truly are and what we are here for (our mission). We don't know our own self.

We are living in a time period where things are moving quickly and creation (manifestation) is easy if you are aligned with who you truly are here to be.

Stop settling for less than what you came here for.
Stop settling for a job you hate or a program you don't resonate with anymore.
Stop settling for the first person who comes along and lust instead of a sacred union.
Stop settling for sickness and low energy instead of health and happiness.

Tap into the truth within you.

Tap into the nudges and synchronicities from god source.

Say it with me out loud so that god can hear you:
"I am free, I am free, I am free!"

The more you go inward, the more your soul rises.
The more your soul rises, the more you are living your soul purpose and why you came to earth at this time.
As you come into higher vibration and alignment with your soul purpose,
the more miracles happen seamlessly and quickly.

The more miracles for you, the more miracles for others.

God wants to give us miracles consistently
but we have to get out of our ego's controlling way and into the flow (creation) state.

So go inward and listen.
It's time to move.

* * *

We are being called by god to take specific actions right now.
Are you listening and doing, or thinking you know best and making excuses?

* * *

"Act, and God will act." - Joan of Arc

Sometimes you have to do the hard thing or the 'impossible' thing in order for miracles to occur.

Do your part, take the action you are resisting or avoiding.
Stop playing how others want you to play.
Stop doing what is expected.

Show god source that you love yourself and are ready to live your highest purpose. The reason you came here at this time.

Only you can act.
Only you can make the decision to love yourself more, regardless of how 'comfortable' your current situation seems.
Only you can show god you are ready.
Nobody else.

Your life, your future, your happiness, your love, your mission - all of it rests within you and your willingness to act upon the guidance god gives you.

* * *

Who are you trusting and believing?
Decisions made out of fear and to follow the crowd "because everyone is doing it!" lead to destruction.
If everyone jumps off the bridge, do you follow?

Trust your soul. Trust in god source.
You will never be led astray.

* * *

You can stop yourself or procrastinate
by being scared of the outcome instead of saying,
"No matter the outcome, I will grow from the process".
#expectations versus #growth

* * *

You can play big or play small.
Criticism can inhibit you or drive you.
Either way, it's your choice.

Don't let shame, guilt, or other low level forms of
manipulation take you off your path.
Keep your vibration high.

* * *

Back in 2002, I was in high school and had just finished
my first oil painting.
My life changed because I knew I had stumbled on one
part of my genius.
I was elated. I was in love with painting!

And I was terrified to pursue it because it was against
everything I had been taught growing up - you have to
work hard to make money, you have to work nine-five,
life is hard, artists live in poverty, blah blah blah.

I applied to art schools anyways and got accepted to
many.

Still finding my way at 18, I listened to everyone else tell me art can't pay my bills and went to a 'normal' university for a 'normal' career path.

I didn't pick up my paint brush for 15 years.
And now? Now I paint for pure joy and love!

* * *

We are no longer in the era of playing it small or hiding our gifts.

You know who you are and why you are here.
It is time to rise
Stop downplaying who YOU are.

* * *

You must be WILLING to surrender
what you think you know, how it's supposed to go, and what you think is your highest path.

Keep the FAITH.
Walk blindly knowing that god source has you!

* * *

What brings you pure, mood elevating, mind altering joy?
Do more of that :)

* * *

It takes strength to know when to ask for help.

Ask and you shall receive.
You've got this!

* * *

Just because you're spiritual/compassionate/helping people doesn't mean that you don't have bills.
Yes, new money systems are being created but until the time that they are in full swing, you must be able to live in the 3D and the 5D.

* * *

The amount of energy, focus, & faith required to live your dreams & fulfill your purpose/mission
is too much for most people.

They don't have the time, energy, or patience.

But you do.
Keep going.

* * *

The Real Battle
The real battle is not sitting isolated in your house keeping your vibration high.
It is out in the world, in the thick of it, amongst other people's energy and in situations that try us.

It is having the self-awareness to hear or see someone and why they are saying or doing what they want - and being able to feel what comes up inside of yourself.

To not be dragged into their energy. To respond as lovingly and firmly as possible. To walk away knowing you did the best you could to keep your vibration high.

Our greatest trials are out in the world - not behind a computer screen, or on a deserted island, or when we are by ourselves doing our spiritual practices at home.

It is the ability to adapt to the curveballs;
to understand that we don't always know why we are led onto a different path than we thought we would be going on;
to feel what we need to feel and then act in our highest good from our own intuition.

It is not in our highest good to stay hidden or surrounded only by like-minded people - the people who need to see our love are usually strangers.

It is not in our highest good to live in another realm because it's easier/more loving, and to not bring the light to the darkest/most fear-ridden places here on earth.

It is not in our highest good to forget that we are the leaders.

We are not doormats and all codependent love givers – we are the warriors of love and we are here to show others that it is possible to live how we live ->
freely and happily (and maybe a bit erratic because our intuition is not always linear).

That it is possible to consciously create your reality - your divine union relationship, your soul work that allows true freedom, your legacy for the next seven generations - with your energy vibration.

Because if we aren't out there, in the thick of it, we are limiting ourselves and our growth.

We are limiting the joy and light we bring to other lives, if only for a few minutes that day. We are limiting our help to Mother Earth and the people living right now.
So it is time to stop hiding.
Time to listen to your intuition.
Time to bring the light.

We are loved, protected, and supported.
We are living and practicing what we talk and post about.
We are love.

And it is time to stand up and shine in all of your glory, all of your gifts, all of your shadows and emotions, all of YOU.
That is what is needed right now.
We need to see and hear YOU.

* * *

Warriors of love (god source) stand firmly in their truth and light.
We laugh right into the face of fear because we have walked through the fires of hell and we fear no evil.
There is only room for love.
Remember who you are.

***

<u>The Differences</u>
I've got one client who taps and meditates, another client who does Buddhist chants, and another who does yoga and journals…

All of them are different yet with the same goal in mind -> letting go/releasing that which no longer serves them - which allows them more connection with god source.

There is no "one way" to get back to god.
There is no "right way" to do it.
No "only way" or else…(fear mongering and shame).

There are as many ways as there are people, because we are each unique with an individual soul blueprint.

I'm grateful that I get to learn from my clients as I guide and teach them. I cater each of their one x one programs to their unique blueprint because it is not a one-size-fits-all world.

Everyone deserves the chance to find their own way, to trust in their own guidance and to have that relationship strengthened with support from someone who's done the work as well.

I used to think many years ago - before any of my many dark nights of the soul/spiritual awakenings - that I knew the right way and that I was right (my ego and arrogance).

Now I know that I am constantly learning and growing, and that the tools I used last year were but a fraction of the tools I use to help my clients today. And the same will be said for next year.

I allow space for my clients to grow.
I help them trust themselves completely and expand in their relationship with source.
Then they uncover their gifts and missions.
Then they take the actions (divine masculine) they are guided to take by their own intuition (divine feminine).

I understand that my way is not the only way, and that the people who are an energetic match for my medicine and guidance become my clients.

If I feel or am told by my intuition that the person needs a different healer/coach/therapist, I direct them to that other healer for all of our highest goods.

My clients become my friends and a part of my tribe. Maybe they had already signed up as part of my soul family before we came here at this time. Or maybe they are a part of my earthly tribe.
That is the beauty of this work; these connections with our soul people.

I am truly grateful that I get to assist some amazing souls at this time of the greatest awakening this planet has ever seen.

* * *

Don't confuse teachers, healers, or entrepreneurs of love and light with having no boundary enforcement (codependency) and not speaking their truth (people pleasing).

They are the first ones to say "No" to anything/anyone that depletes their energy and mission.

* * *

I hope you take the break that you need.
Yes, from your phone and social media too; you're not missing out on anything.
What is meant for you is there, or you will be told by your intuition the actions to take to create it.

* * *

I am holding you accountable ->
wake up and use your gifts.
The time is now.
We are all here.
I banish anything stopping you from fulfilling your mission and using your gifts.

* * *

We all have our soul missions, but that doesn't mean we can't co-create and build with others.
Say it out loud with joy: I call in my soul tribe, my soul coworkers, my soul employees, etc. to assist me.
Now get ready!

* * *

Reminder: When you're about to level up (move on to the next chapter of your life), you're given two options. One is to propel you forward (looks crazy/you feel fear) and one will keep you on your previous level (safe and comfy).
Discernment is key.

* * *

When you are living from your soul, your heart, your truth, YOU will trigger people who have healing to do (but who don't truly want to change their habits/beliefs) and you will inspire those who are growing and striving to have total freedom.
Keep shining!

* * *

Learn to distinguish between true friends and people you've outgrown.
Only you can follow your mission and create your life.
The people who you surround yourself with reflect on you and are reflections of you.

* * *

Residual energy is real.
When we upgrade, there are still issues to go through/clear.
But you are so much further ahead than you were six, even two-three, months ago.

Keep going!

* * *

It is okay to unfollow, unfriend, or remove people in your life who you no longer resonate with.

Who you were six months ago is different from today.
We are upgrading quickly.
Raise your vibe.

* * *

As you elevate,
beware the distractions to get you off your mission.
They take your focus.
They drain your energy.

These include: passive aggressive comments on anything you say or post, rude dm's or texts, manipulative messages or comments to make you feel guilt or shame, etc.

You are a sovereign being and you do not tolerate disrespect - in physical life or online.

You are here for love and living in the reality you create.
And creating that reality requires your focus and energetic boundaries.

Remember who you are.
Keep shining.
I love you.

* * *

<u>Chaos and Turmoil</u>
Through turmoil we understand what we will do to live; what we will do for those we love to live; what we will sacrifice to continue breathing.
We understand ourselves on a deeper human level.

Will we be influenced by fear mongering and hatred, thus spewing negativity into our world and those around us? Sacrificing our inner knowing and collectively creating more war?

Or will we continue on the path of love, consciously creating a new way?
Clearing the energies, and focusing on the mission?

Because there will be casualties - on both human and soul levels - while the old systems are crumbling.

This isn't just about sending thoughts and prayers. This is about your vibration. Holding your energetic vibration. Holding your integrity. Holding your truth.

Knowing that war is never the answer. Knowing that there are lies and false energy around every current event. Knowing that this is creating trauma, adding to more than what was already created these past three years, the past 100 years.

And understanding that we are here to continue clearing that trauma. To continue lighting the path.

To continue clearing the spiritual warfare.
To continue using our imagination (our thoughts) and our actions to create a world of love and peace.

We do not buy into the propaganda.
We do not sell our souls to fear and conflict.

We are the warriors of light.
We stay the course.
For the highest good of all.

* * *

<u>There is No Competition.</u>
My story, and especially my sacred union with my husband, is to inspire you.

To help you see that there is a different way to live and be.
That not everything can be planned out.
That we must truly walk in blind faith.

Because this life I am living now (and for the past four years) - it is the road less traveled.

It is a break from the norm (false matrix).

I never thought I would be on this path.
I never knew there was a love as deep as this; a love as deep as I love myself and god.

But now I know.
Now I only move in faith -> in complete trust to that ever-knowing source, to god.

That is not to say that I don't have tough days; we all do.
Some days my body aches or I didn't sleep well, or have trouble feeling gratitude.

But the idea is to center back to my heart, back to my breath, back to source.
To use my imagination to continue creating the life I desire.

Because if I can dream it and create it, so can you.
In collaboration with your heart, your intuition, your faith in the unknown (the impossible), and god.
You have the power.
You are the creator of your life.

You signed up for this journey and to also lead the way, for the highest good.

Remember who you are.
You are amazing and you are ready!

* * *

We are not here to collapse and lose heart.
We are here to lead the way.

Remember why you are here.
Do activities that keep your vibration high.
We have helped other planets transition before.

Keep the faith.
Stay the course.

* * *

Your intentions (goals/prayers/etc.) must be clear and grounded in your soul.
Communicate with your highest self, create for your highest good, and remember that you are love and that everything is possible!

* * *

Don't put yourself in a box with labels.
You are multidimensional.
You are allowed to talk about whatever, and show up however, your truth dictates.
You are free. You are free. You are free!

* * *

What you are doing this month might be different from what you did last month.
What you do after high energy days might be completely different than today.
Expand, receive, & remember that you are loved and protected.
For your highest good.

* * *

<u>You Know Your Boundaries</u>
My husband and I are both very stubborn.
Not in a negative way where we are obstinate about our opinions.

More in the - these are my boundaries and this is my integrity type of way.
Which is hilarious if we 'argue'.

We are very in sync and telepathic, and there is no ego. And this means we have rarely 'argued' due to how similar we are at a soul level.

We both listen because he is a reflection of me and I am of him. And we both live in integrity.

There might be discomfort at discussing a topic, followed by growth.
But there's never disrespect or dishonor, rage or yelling, crying or projection.
Our divine union mission is love and that is our example in this world.

You might notice (especially obvious now), that the collective wounds are in plain sight now. That people entrenched in the false matrix/3D system are doubling down on their toxic and trauma behaviors.
The refusal to change their habits meanwhile expecting new and magical things to happen for them (definition of insanity).

The willingness to ignore all of the signs despite the natural laws -> for example three signs consecutively such as losing a job or house, car breaking down, husband/wife leaving, purse stolen, health issues, etc.
Huge life signs asking them to wake up.

So when they run into you (or us), they are immediately triggered or try to project guilt/shame/victimhood/poverty onto you.

They can't understand why or how you are so free and so happy. How you radiate love and joy.
How you always see a solution to an 'issue' or see a blessing in disguise.
How you are unwilling to compromise your values and boundaries no matter how they might push or scream or cry.
Or manipulate or get passive aggressive or what have you.

When your soul is free and you know your mission, you maintain focus on your purpose and consciously creating your life. That is your energy, your currency.

There's no judgment coming from you, no way to be dragged into their drama or gossip, no time for insecurities and low self-esteem/worth.
Nor will you tolerate disrespect, lies, and non-responsibility.

The stubbornness in you is a commitment to yourself and what you came here to do - your agreement with god -> before all others.
So you detach yourself completely, keep them at extreme arm's length or remove them from your life - and you keep going.

Sometimes we stand alone in our truth and sometimes we have a partner, close family member, or close friend who stands with us.
Yet we are not alone.

We know that we are loved and protected.

And we are simply unwilling to waver when it comes to building the new earth -> where every single person stands in integrity and truth, love and joy, freedom and peace.

Which in turn is just the example that people need right now.
You are here, you are here, you are here!

* * *

Your skills, your gifts, your interests –
they are all evolving right now.
Be open to the changes. Be open to what is being removed.
Open your heart up even wider.
You are a magnificent being!

* * *

Your life and the world you create is your work of art.
You are the portal.
You leave the energy trail for others to live freely and to be love.

* * *

<u>Let Me Re-Introduce Myself</u>
My name is Acacia and I'm from Kansas, USA.
I went to school in Texas, lived in NYC for 11 years and then Bali for two.

Now, I reside in Scotland with my amazing husband.

My first ever book writing group "The Book Finishers" in summer 2022 was a success, and the second one was too!
I also offer 1x1 Book Writing Consultations and editing. I'm so honored to help others create, write, and edit their first book.
The new earth needs new voices, books and stories!

I currently offer Divine Union 1:1 sessions to bring your divine union into the physical world.
My first published book, "My Past Lives and How They Came Back to Haunt Me" was written in streams of consciousness on ten of my past lives, and I followed my intuition in every aspect of the book process.
I also write short stories for fun.

My second book (which you are now reading) is called "Daily Doses of Inspiration: Volume 1 – For Spiritual Seekers" and it is to give motivation to those newly on the spiritual journey, to know they aren't alone and that it's worth it!

My third book will be underway in spring 2023, and that thrills me! (Hint: it's about my Divine Union)

I also paint oil paintings in three different areas: female nudes (with no faces), old men, and flowers. I've just started taking a painting class again to hold myself accountable for making time for this gift of mine.

Over the past four years, I've coached people with
trauma, through divorce/relationship/job changes,
mindset resets, (re)discovering their purpose, and healing
their inner masculine/feminine and relationship with
god/creator/source.
I'm also a yoga instructor, energy healer/mover, soul
code activator, and nutritionist/healthy living teacher.

I thrive on learning new things and have started
exploring my Akashic Records as well as opening up to
more gifts from my starseed origin and other planetary
lives.

My focus (my energy) is on creating the life I came here
to live - a life that I love and that is in service to the
highest good.
I've come to trust my intuition and god completely
(when I don't trust them, it's a hard lesson).

I move in grace, joy, love, and compassion. I healed
myself of severe anxiety and severe depression. I healed
my trauma, integrated my shadows, and built
relationships with my inner masculine and feminine.

It took a lot of hard work and focus to get to where I am
today. I cut people out of my life who were leeching my
energy. I left situations that were dragging me down.
I put myself first -> for the first time in my life!

And now I can say that I'm on my divine path and
missions (because I signed up for quite a few!).
As within, so without.
I'm doing it! I'm creating every experience I have.

Every joyful and loving moment.

That's not to say there aren't curveballs - there are - but I don't collapse and get defensive or negative or think the world is ending. I look at it, feel whatever comes up, and say, "I strengthen my faith in myself and my mission".

So welcome to my community! Feel free to look around on my FB or my website, and check out my art and my life. Stay around, get comfy, comment or message me with any questions.

I love getting to know people and it's important to connect. Human connection is special and it's what we're here for as well as our missions.

This is the Earth 'School'
Have a wonderful day and remember ->
you are loved and protected.
You are here for a reason.
You are love :)

* * *

Keep speaking your truth
Keep shining.
We are with you.

* * *

<u>The Warrior Dream</u>
An angel came and said, "You are a Warrior of Light."

"What weapons do I need to fight this battle?"

"I am giving you the Sword of Truth." He handed over a glowing, pulsating blue sword. "The sword connects you with the ultimate truth. This sword goes from your sacral chakra to your throat chakra, creating a clear channel of communication of the truth."

"But I must also need something to protect myself with?"

The angel replied, "Yes, here is the Shield of Faith. It will protect you. Have faith in what you say and do as the truth. Nothing can stop you when you are truly connected to faith."

And he gave over the glowing white shield.

The Warriors of Truth have been activated.
This is even more apparent in a Divine Union but is happening to the bringers of truth.

We call in the other Warriors of Truth.
Rally around each other.
Offer help and assistance as you are guided to.

"We are here, we are here, we are here.
We are activated into our true timeline.
We are free, we are warriors, and we are protected.
Our voices shall be heard and the truth will be spoken with the sword of truth.
The shield of faith protects us.

We know we move in divine guidance and we surrender
to the divine plan.
And so it is."

* * *

Abundance in the New Earth is for all.
But you must take the aligned actions.
Align with your soul.
Align with your truth.
You are the receiver.

* * *

<u>Tests of Faith</u>
We are being asked to remove all old and stale energy to allow the new to come in.

This means removing old material objects (i.e. art, books, furniture…), old beliefs/thought patterns that limit you and your creations, and people who don't believe in you or resonate with you.
Then you can allow / receive the new soul aligned people, objects, and beliefs.
You can then receive more of your gifts, more energy for service to the highest good, and more abundance in all areas of your life.

Feel into the energy of the object, thought, or person and ask yourself if it serves your highest good.
Release it with love (donate the object, transmute the energy of the thought/belief, and let the person move onto others that align to their highest good).

Letting go makes room for the new.
Are you willing to allow the new energy in?
Remember that:
You are multidimensional.
You are the creator of your life and reality.
You are limitless and free.
You are love.

* * *

You are tested so that
you can let go of old beliefs/thoughts,
hold more energy and expand.

Dig even deeper into your faith and
see the test for what it is.

You are a multidimensional being!
You are limitless!
Expand even more.

* * *

To-Do List for Soul Mission

Write the answers down on this page, or in a separate journal specifically for manifesting.

1) What brings you joy to do? List three things.

   _____

   _____

   _____

2) What would you do every day if you could?

   _____

   _____

   _____

3) What did you do (that was your favorite thing to do) as a child? What did you want to be when you were age six-ten?

_____

_____

_____

_____

4) Take all that you enjoy, what you loved doing as a kid, and ask yourself what you truly want to do in your life? Now imagine yourself doing this. This is your soul speaking to you. *(Your soul mission can change or evolve, it's about taking the steps towards doing what brings you joy!)*

_____

_____

_____

To Further Your Spiritual Aspect

Along with the questions at the end of each section, there are other ways to deepen your spiritual side (aspect). The goal is self-sovereignty and self-love.

1) Protect your energy daily by strengthening your energetic field (aura) by saying the following prayer out loud (or a variation of it): "Guides/ancestors/guardian angels/god source, please protect my energy field today (or while I sleep). I call back all of my energy and power to myself right now."

2) Build up your own knowing – your intuition by taking one day per week to allow it to guide every action you take. Ask your intuition (you can place your hand on your heart) what you should wear, what you should eat, what you should do in this moment. Listen, and take action on what your intuition says. Your power comes from being able to trust yourself (your intuition) 100%.

3) Sit in complete silence, in whatever position is comfortable for you, with your phone and computer off, for three-five minutes/day, with your eyes closed. Learn to simply BE. *Train yourself to do this. You have control over your body and mind – not the other way around!*

4)   Daily gratitude list to flip your mind and how you think. List three-five things you are grateful for as soon as you wake up or go to sleep. Of course, do this more when you feel like it. *Gratitude raises your energetic vibration and attracts that vibration towards you.* Oprah claims this is the number one way to manifest and change your life ☺

5)   Continue investing in yourself (and your mission). If you enjoyed art classes as a child, go take an art class. If you enjoy cooking, go learn how to cook a new cuisine with others. If you enjoy languages or dancing, do it! If you're building a business, you employ a business coach. Etc.

6)   Remembering who you truly are with past life work, multidimensional work, and shadow work. I highly recommend calling in (manifesting) a healer who you are aligned with (ask your higher self to assist you) to help you in these areas.

If you want to explore more of these areas in depth, including doing your soul work/mission, aligning with your true self or writing your book(s) that you know you're here to write, please feel free to book a 15 minute Discovery Call with me via my website at www.byacacia.com.

I am here to assist you in your own self-sovereignty and remembrance of who you truly are.

You are more powerful than you realize! It's time for you to rise!

For any feedback or questions, contact me via my website or my Facebook page.

Sending you much love, clarity, and peace.
Acacia

About the Author

Deeply knowing that she was strange from a young age, Acacia has repeatedly taken the road less traveled. Having read all of the books in her grade school library, she tackled high school books and the public library by age 11.

Heavily influenced by Hemingway, Fitzgerald, the Brontës, Bukowski, and others, she began writing short stories at age ten and dreamed of writing a book while sitting barefoot in the tops of trees at her family's home in Kansas.

After an 11 year career in NYC, Acacia headed to Bali following a severe burnout that left her questioning why she was on earth. Her winding spiritual path led her back to her writing and oil painting, fluidly combining with years of coaching people and teaching yoga.

This book was created from her social media posts, talks, and live interviews, along with messages she shared with her clients on their own spiritual seeking journeys.

Acacia is currently working on Daily Doses of Inspiration - Volume 2 while she hosts private book writing groups and continues coaching Divine Union Alignment clients.

For more information or to contact Acacia, please go to www.byacacia.com or her Facebook page at www.facebook.com/acacia.lawson.3.

Printed in Great Britain
by Amazon